P9-DXI-978

"As a beginner I need this book. Next to my helmet and wrist guards, it's my best safety gear and almost as good as a personal instructor!"

ROBERT CAMPBELL
BEGINNING SKATER

"*Get Rolling* goes into instructional detail that works. I bring my reading glasses to the parking lots now (heaven forbid!) and I read and skate until I get it. Thank you Liz. We will be fit in our fifties without a doubt."

JIM FINK — WENT FROM *GET ROLLING* TO SPEED SKATING IN 2 YEARS
SEATTLE, WA

"Skaters will love this book! It takes you from beginner to expert."

KEN TROTTA
BEGINNING SKATER

"A very, very heartfelt thanks to you. I re-read the book every time I need to summon up guts and psyche myself."

KAMALA E. SARMA
BEGINNING SKATER

"I know one thing: reading this book helped me a lot. I had an idea, a plan of action, moves to practice, and goals to meet."

LAURIE BOZANICH
BEGINNING SKATER AND ALL-ROUND ATHLETE

"Anyone taking up the sport should read *Get Rolling*."

HARRY STROBEL
IN-LINE SEPTUAGENARIAN AND SPORTING GOOGS RETAILER

"Congratulations! *Get Rolling* is a masterpiece."

ROBERT O. NAEGELE, JR.
IISA PRESIDENT EMERITUS, PAST CHAIRMAN OF THE BOARD, ROLLERBLADE, INC.

i

"*Get Rolling* will provide necessary information at a time when many are looking to increase their skills and find new skating challenges. In fact, some of your information was used at this weekend's [in-line instructor training] workshop."

> Joe Janasz
> Former Executive Director
> International In-line Skating Association

"Really enjoyed *Get Rolling*. I found it interesting, very readable, and easy to understand. The book's pep talks are a welcome tone for someone just starting out and scared to death."

> Dwayne Hebda
> Sports Information Director
> United States Amateur Confederation of Roller Skating

"Clear, simple illustrations and other user-friendly touches make this instructional and safety manual readily digestible."

> Henry Berry, Editor/Publisher
> *The Small Press Book Review*

"This guide is jam-packed with information, accompanied by clean drawings and illustrations...with some helpful tips on techniques and suggestions for drills."

> Daniel J. Levinson, History and English Teacher
> From a review in *Kliatt Young adult Paperback Book Guide*

"The basics of the lessons are sound. Given the growing popularity of in-line skating, consider this book for older students."

> Sherry Hoy
> The Book Report, a Journal for High School Librarians

Get Rolling

Get Rolling

THE BEGINNER'S
GUIDE TO IN-LINE SKATING

Third Edition

Written and illustrated by Liz Miller

Photographs by Dan Kibler

Enjoy wheel life!
Liz Miller

GET ROLLING BOOKS
DANVILLE, CALIFORNIA

GET ROLLING BOOKS
DANVILLE, CALIFORNIA

First edition published by Pix & Points, Union City, CA; ISBN 0-9632196-2-6

Second edition published by Ragged Mountain Press, Camden ME; ISBN 0-07-043258-9

ISBN 0-9632196-3-4

Library of Congress Control Number: 2003090911

Edited by Dan Kibler, Ann Greenleaf and Kathryn Mallien

Book design based on the second edition by Molly Mulhen Gross, Ragged Mountain Press

Questions regarding book contents or ordering should be addressed to:

Get Rolling Books, PO Box 1115, Danville, CA 94526; 925-323-0486. www.getrolling.com

Warning

This book is intended to educate and encourage the beginning and intermediate recreational
in-line skater. The author has attempted to make it as informative and accurate as possible;
however, there may be mistakes. Therefore, it should be considered a reference and not the
final word on the sport of in-line skating. Skaters are strongly encouraged to wear knee and
elbow pads, wrist guards and, especially, a helmet at all times, and to obey all recommended
safety rules. Before starting an in-line training regimen, be sure to consult your physician.
The author and publisher take no responsibility and are not liable for any person who is
injured while using in-line skates.

To my mom,

Gerry Miller, who once said, "Honey we're not laughing *at* you, we're laughing *with* you!"

Acknowledgements

Each edition of *Get Rolling* has been a labor of love fueled by endorphins and a touch of caffeine. This book evolved from day to day and edition to edition thanks to the morning coffee in bed, steady patience, and hours of work delivered by my life partner, web master and mentor Dan Kibler.

I wouldn't be fully qualified to write about this subject without a solid instructional base. The IISA's Inline Certification Program gave me expert training for teaching beginner and intermediate skaters, but even better, for analyzing their learning stumbling blocks. I've watched the organization grow to promote the sport the world over, and I'm proud to be a 10-year beneficiary of their services and programs.

Thanks also to the ICP's many dedicated instructors and examiners, who over the years provided input to the development of my drills and whose passion keeps this wonderful sport alive and growing.

I owe a big thank you to two very photogenic fellow instructors, Mireille Kennedy and Lester Leong, who donated their time, patience, and willingness to demonstrate the in-line skills for the photos in these pages.

Guiding and instructing for Zephyr Inline Adventures' tours and five-day Learn-to-Skate camps has been invaluable for formalizing my own instruction techniques, leadership and professionalism. Allan Wright, owner and founder, is a consummate skate professional and I'm very grateful for our association.

But most of all, I am deeply indebted to the hundreds of students who were partners in the development of my lessons and drills. Thanks to them, I've been able to constantly refine my teaching approach and my ability to articulate the moves required to learn each skill. And every year, my students and I experience more revelations to make learning how to in-line skate even more fun, safe and easy!

Contents

Preface

I was giddy with excitement that day in 1991 as I caromed down the wide, carpeted hall at work to show my boss my brand new purple, green and fuchsia in-line skates.

Looking back from today's perspective, it seems perfectly logical that a software technical writer with desktop publishing skills and an athletic, outdoors lifestyle would want to document the moves that lead to success on in-lines. But if I had known that this first roll down the hall would led to a future of writing, illustrating, and self-publishing in-line skating books that have already touched the lives of thousands of new and experienced skaters all over the world, I would have stopped mid-lurch and taken a big gulp!

Though I had been terribly intrigued by the sport, I'd hesitated for a year, wondering if I really could learn how to in-line skate without maiming myself (or worse, my pride!) for life. But my first moments on those colorful, plastic boots made it clear that the months of wondering and worrying without actually trying on a pair of in-lines were months of skating fun I'd never get back.

My coordination wasn't what I'd hoped it would be on outdoors pavement, though. Skating forward turned out to be a breeze, but there were scary parts. As a 40-year-old novice, I was chagrined by my lack of confidence and strong feeling of vulnerability. How could an experienced alpine skier be so afraid of crashing? I was terrified at the prospect of speeding out of control. Even the flattest looking parking lots had a slope, always pulling me unwillingly toward a gutter or drain. During those first days, that speed felt like terminal velocity!

Since I could find no suitable instruction books or lessons at the time, it was through my own analytical abilities and body awareness that I began to gain skill and confidence on wheels. My enthusiasm grew as fast as my coordination, and I soon became convinced that with the proper guidance, just about *any* reasonably fit person can learn in-line skating.

My mission became clear: to tell the whole world about this wonderful form of fitness, fun and family recreation! That's how the first edition of *Get Rolling* was born. A few months after it came out, I was proud to learn that my words were used by the International In-line Skating Association's new Inline Certification Program (ICP) to develop a standard teaching method. Soon, I too, was certified to instruct others, sharing with my own students the mutually gratifying experience of an in-line skate lesson.

Over a decade later, I am still dedicated to helping people get rolling safely. In teaching, I share my joy and skills with hundreds of beginning and intermediate skaters every year. Most of them come to me with at least as much hesitation as I had back in 1991. I love empowering new skaters, especially the ever-growing number of beginners over 35 years old.

I wrote *Get Rolling* for you: isn't it about time you took up the in-line lifestyle? Who knows, it might steer *your* life in a marvelous new direction too!

Happy skating!

Introduction

What's new in this edition

The third edition of *Get Rolling* reflects my perspectives on in-line skating gained through a decade of continuous involvement with the sport.

Today I have more experience and compassion than ever as your personal in-line tutor, with two certifications from the International In-Line Skating Association's Inline Certification Program (IISA/ICP) and 10 years of teaching under my belt. This book stands out from others not only because of its adherence to the ICP standards used worldwide, but for another quality that remains unchanged from the first edition: *Get Rolling* still approaches the sport with unparalleled empathy for the apprehensive beginning skater.

To make your path to success more clear, each major skill in this edition is introduced with a brief overview such as this example from the In-line Fundamentals section:

What it is: Stances, terms, falling, getting up.
How to learn: Eight mini-lessons on the carpet.

The instructions in the Beginning Skills and Intermediate Skills chapters are based on the ICP's teaching methods. When called for, I introduce the move with non-rolling preparatory exercises. Each skating movement is described in a step-by-step approach, followed by related mobility drills and practice tips for conquering common learning problems.

Following that same format, I have added a few new drills in this third edition, developed from years of observing how people learn. I also added a section on Yoga for skaters because the poses can be very effective for increasing balance and strength as well as for stretching tight muscles after a long roll. I have experienced all of these benefits firsthand.

As you progress through the lessons in this book, you are sure to "get roll-igion," and begin to hunger for new places to explore on your in-lines. You will find advice about where to discover great skating tours wherever you go, and how to stay safe skating at night, with large groups, alone in the countryside and, of course, near automobiles.

Chapter summaries

Chapter 1 - Get Ready to Roll: Read a brief sport history and discover just a few of the benefits of in-line skating. There are tips on pre-skate strategies for success and cross references to the skills to focus on if you are interested in pursuing a specific in-line discipline later on.

Chapter 2 - Avoiding Injury: Understand what's involved in choosing to skate safely: wearing protective gear, learning the basics, adopting an expert's attitude, physical fitness, and maintaining your equipment.

Chapter 3 - Getting Equipped: Learn about proper fit and features to consider when buying skates and protective gear for yourself or your child. Plan ahead for skating in different weather conditions and consider what to pack in your skater's gear bag.

Chapter 4 - Beginning Skills: Learn the eight beginning in-line skills (including how to stop!) by experiencing the body positions first standing still, then gradually adding the movements through a sequence of building drills and balance exercises.

Chapter 5 - Intermediate Skills: Learn fifteen intermediate skills through stationary and rolling drills, then practice them using mobility and balance exercises. Tackle four impressive tricks and learn how to deal with common urban obstacles.

Chapter 6 - Advanced Slaloms: Learn to love downhill skating by practicing drills that will help you enjoy the pull of gravity.

Chapter 7 - Getting Fit with Roll-Aerobics: Learn where and how to use fitness skating to get an aerobic workout on your in-lines, how to track your heart rate, and how to warm up and cool down for a good cardiovascular work out.

Chapter 8 - Great Places to Skate: Discover the locations in every town where fun skating is likely to be found, plus invaluable safety tips about skating on bike routes, road shoulders, in groups, and at night.

How to use this book

Here's how to get rolling as quickly and safely as possible:

- Don't skip the Avoiding Injury chapter (starting on page 35)!
- If you are taking up in-line skating so you can participate in a discipline such as roller hockey or speedskating, review the building blocks section at the end of the first chapter, "Get Ready to Roll" (page 32), to find out which skills serve as your intended sport's building blocks. Then concentrate particularly on those skills as you are learning them, sticking to the sequence presented in this book.
- Make sure to do the "Before you roll" drills before proceeding to the rolling versions. These prepare you both mentally and physically for experiencing a new skill.

- Take the time to read, rehearse, and visualize the steps in each lesson before trying them on skates. This will start you out on surer footing.
- Before any skating session, and especially before attempting anything new, skate a few practice laps for ten minutes to warm up your muscles and review the moves you've already learned.
- If not otherwise specified, assume all new pointers for turning are based on a *counterclockwise* direction, because that is the direction most people favor.
- We all favor one leg over the other, making it easier to learn new skills more easily on one side than the other. Once you've mastered a technique on your easy side, don't forget to work harder on your more difficult side.
- After you learn a new skill, practice it often to improve not only that feat but your balance, coordination and confidence, too.

Key Terms

A-frame Stance: A balanced, upright stance with skates positioned parallel and wider than shoulder width. "Frame" means your whole body is shaped like the capital letter A.

A-Stance: A version of the ready position where the toes are nearly touching and the heels are angled out. In this stance, your skates form the A.

ABEC: A bearing precision rating system developed by the Annular Bearing Engineering Council. An ABEC 5 bearing spins easier than an ABEC 1.

action leg: The leg that performs the work for a given movement (e.g., kicking a ball), as opposed to the balance leg, which provides support.

axle guide: A frame component that can be rotated in some skate models to allow *rockering* of the wheels or lengthening of the wheel base.

balance: One of the four fundamentals of skating, balance on in-lines is achieved through proper stance. Good balance results in better equilibrium and confidence for learning new skills.

bearings: The hardware that makes a smooth-spinning wheel (two per wheel), consisting of small ball bearings that roll in a track called the *race*.

carving: The act of riding one or both sets of wheel edges around the curved arc of a turn, commonly used in describing Slalom Turns.

center edge: The place on the wheel that is in contact with the pavement when the skate is perpendicular to the surface.

centerline: An imaginary line that runs down the middle of your path of travel.

coasting ready position: The rolling stance that results after the skater strides to attain a moderate speed (enough momentum to ensure good balance), and then relaxes into a balanced ready position.

coned: The shaved-off state of a wheel that is worn on one side, indicating the wheel needs to be flipped over and rotated or replaced.

core: See *hub*.

corresponding edges: The outside edge of the right skate's wheels corresponds to the inside edge of the left skate's wheels, and vice versa. When both skates are tipped in the same direction, they are said to be on corresponding edges.

cross training: Using in-line skating workouts to enhance performance for another sport, and vice versa.

cuff: The portion of the in-line skate that encases the ankle, usually plastic, often hinged at the ankle.

cuff-activated braking: A braking method using a special arm-mounted brake that can be engaged by pressing the boot cuff back as the skate is pushed forward with all four wheels in contact with the pavement.

diameter: The measurement that determines wheel sizes, usually printed on the side of the wheel in millimeters.

durometer: A rating system used to classify in-line wheel hardness, usually printed on the side of the wheel with a two-digit number followed by the letter A. The higher the number, the harder the wheel.

edges: The portion of the wheel that contacts the pavement. There are three edges on a skate's wheels: The inside edge, outside edge and center edge.

edging: The act of tipping the skate onto the outside or inside edge to perform skating movements. Edging is one of the key fundamentals of in-line skating.

fall line: An imaginary line from the top of a hill to the bottom, along which gravity has the strongest pull.

footbed: The replaceable insole of the skate boot liner.

frame: The chassis attached to the sole of the in-line boot into which the wheels are bolted (custom frames can be purchased for some skate models).

gliding: The rolling of a skate on the pavement after a stroke.

grinding: A trick that involves landing on the skate's wheel frame between the wheels, usually to slide across the edge of a tree planter or down a stairway bannister; also performed on special apparatus during aggressive skating competitions.

Half Swizzle: A forward or backward Swizzle performed with one action leg only; the other leg remains the support leg. Also known as scooters or sculling.

hub: A hard substance in the wheel's core that the urethane bonds to, providing a stable seat for the bearings.

inside edges: The sides of the wheels below the inside arch of the foot.

outside edges: The sides of the wheels below the outside of the foot.

polyurethane: The plastic material used to manufacture in-line wheels; also referred to as simply *urethane*.

pressure: The application of pressure is one of the key fundamentals of in-line skating. Pressure application results in a wide range of skating skills when it is combined with rotation, weight transfer and edging.

profile: The wheel's shape when viewed from the edge. Wide profiles result in quick-turning, slower skates; the narrowest profiled wheels are used for speed.

race: The track inside a bearing around which the balls roll.

ready position: The balanced alignment of the body that results in equilibrium and confidence. Feet are shoulder width apart. Shoulders, hip joints and arches are balanced along an invisible line that runs from head to foot. Knees and hips are flexed, hands and arms are at waist height within sight.

recovery: The act of returning the skate that has just finished a stroke to the proper position to push off into a new stroke.

rockered: The center wheels are slightly lower than the end wheel. The resulting "curved blade" gives the skater more turning maneuverability (used in hockey and figure skating).

rotation: Rotary motion is one of the key fundamentals of in-line skating. Upper body rotation is used to help skaters learn most turning skills.

Safe-T: The stance used for standing still. The brakeless heel is rolled up against the other skate's inner foot.

shield: The exterior cover on the side of a bearing; may be permanent or removable for maintenance.

skitching: Hitching a ride by grabbing onto a moving vehicle: don't do it!.

spacer: The metal or plastic unit that sits within the hub between the bearings.

Stride One: The beginning stride, which consists of short strokes with toes pointed out; used to introduce beginners to stroking and gliding and also to skate safely over wet or rough surfaces.

Stride Two: The basic in-line stride used for forward propulsion.

Stride Three: The power stride, which combines an aerodynamic body position with an enhanced stroke to maximize power and efficiency; used by fitness and speed skaters.

striding: The result of combining stroking and gliding.

stroking: The leg action that propels the skater in forward or backward movement.

support leg: The leg that provides support and bears the most weight during movements that require independent legwork; also known as the balance leg.

T-Stop: An advanced stopping method accomplished by dragging one skate's wheels across the pavement.

urethane: See *polyurethane*.

V-Stance: A version of the ready position where the heels are nearly touching and the toes are pointed out.

wheel base: The length of a skate's wheel contact with the pavement.

wheel frame: The chassis attached to the sole of the in-line boot into which the wheels are bolted (custom frames can be purchased for some skate models).

CHAPTER 1

Get Ready to Roll

In-Line skating is for you!

Most of us had the opportunity to roll around on a pair of skates as youngsters. And, like most things kids do, it was fun. Whether outdoors or at a rink, we delighted in the thrill of physical movement, a touch of speed, or just being with our friends. Then we grew up.

WHO SKATES?

Everybody who picks up this book has one thing in common: you are intrigued by in-line skating. You may have youngsters of your own now. You may be single or part of a couple. You might be deeply committed to attaining a career goal or to making the most of your leisure hours. You may be a couch spud or a frustrated jock; in the prime of your life or in your "golden years."

The good news is that just about everybody who is interested in in-line skating is capable of enjoying the sport to its fullest.

Whoever you are, why *haven't* you tried in-line skating yet? Perhaps you harbor one of the common doubts:

- What if I hurt myself, or worse, look like an idiot on wheels?
- It must take a long time and a lot of falls to get good enough to have fun.
- It will be too hard to control my speed or stop on those things.
- I'm middle aged—way too old for such nonsense!

Fitness enthusiasts may have other reservations. You already have a regular routine to stay in shape, or a specific sport or hobby that requires physical training. You may see in-line skating as physical, but your concerns are about its cross training value:

- Is it strenuous enough to get my heartbeat up to aerobic training rate?
- How can anything that looks so fun be a good workout?
- Can cross training on skates complement my skiing, biking, running, or (your sport here)?

While more and more people of all kinds are taking up in-line skating, athletes were the first. The ice hockey players in Minnesota who designed the prototypes for today's in-line skates enjoyed their "dry-land" cross training so much they started skating for fun, and soon began to share the recreation with their friends. Before long, in-line skates were being mass produced, and more and more skiers, bicyclists, speed skaters, rowers and many other athletes were using them to cross train.

Now in-line skating itself has generated several new competitive sports: extreme down hill races; endurance and short track speed events; street and ramp ("vert") competitions; and, of course, roller hockey, to name the most popular. Apolo Anton Ohno, 2002 Olympic short track gold medalist, transitioned from in-line racing to the ice.

Because in-line skating is so easy to learn, convenient, and beneficial to the body, the number of non athletes the sport attracts exploded in the mid-1990s. People of all ages are no longer intimidated by the misconception that only the fearless or young can learn to skate on a single row of wheels. And they've all come to realize that every moment of pre-skating hesitation turned out to be lost skating time.

- A well-made skate boot has such good ankle support that first-timers are instantly mobile.

- The learning curve for in-line skating basics is incredibly short compared to that for such sports as skiing, wind surfing, and tennis.

- Skating allows great freedom of movement without restrictive body positions, such as those necessary when riding a bike or using an aerobics apparatus.

- In-line skating complements the "eat your broccoli" forms of exercise: besides keeping your body fit and burning calories, it's also invigoratingly fun.

WHY DO WE SKATE?

The big question is, why are so many people falling in love with their in-line skates? Here are just a few reasons.

- In-line skates are portable and versatile. You can strap them on for a lunch hour jaunt or for a refreshing evening roll around your neighborhood. You can keep them in the trunk of your car for the spontaneous whim or pack them as part of your business travel kit.

- Safety on skates can be learned, just like the other skills. Armed with protective gear, the basic moves and a few important safety tips, every beginner can learn to skate with confidence.

- Skating is sociable. When skaters congregate from all over the area at the local skating "scene" they are eager to share the skating experience and their own techniques. It's easy to make new friends on skates.

- You can enjoy in-line skating without fear of joint stress. The fluid strokes of the forward glide can produce a training heart rate, providing an alternative to high-impact aerobic activities like jogging.

- In-line skating improves balance, strengthens every muscle from the lower back to the knees, and stimulates the upper body.

- Used for cross training, in-line skating is a welcome change from specific and repetitive workouts geared toward improved sports-related performance.

- In these times of purposeful pursuits, in-line skating provides a guilt-free excuse to have fun. Studies have shown that the ability to have fun is a requirement to being a well-adjusted person!

In-line skating captures a special kinesthetic joy that comes from unrestricted physical movement. Its stroke and glide are almost effortless and instinctive, giving you the freedom to abandon yourself to the joy of physical expression. The day you try in-line skating, you will find that within minutes after taking those first tentative strokes, you will be laughing and excited and eager for more. You will feel like a kid again.

> **TIPS FOR SKATING IN THE WORLD**
> Make sure you can get back down whatever you skate up.

WHAT ARE THE PHYSICAL REQUIREMENTS?

You do not need extraordinary balance skills, muscular strength, previous skating experience, aerobic capacity, a stint with the circus, or youth to experience the benefits of in-line skating. A pair of reasonably fit legs is all it takes: if you can climb to your feet from hands and knees without grabbing onto something to pull you up, you are ready to roll. (See "Physical fitness" on page 41.)

As with any activity more strenuous than walking, you must be aware of your physical limitations before starting to skate. If you have a chronic illness or skeletal problems, make sure you talk to your family doctor about your interest in in-line skating before you invest in a pair of your own skates.

If you have not had a check up recently, now is the time to get one. After you spend several months regularly in-line skating, you and your doctor will both be impressed when you compare your improved "after" with your "before" condition.

HOW LONG DOES IT TAKE TO GET GOOD?

Your internal gyroscope has been constantly improving since you first began to walk. Every balance activity you ever learned is still with you to ease your in-line schooling. This is the reason many people can still ride a bicycle decades after their last opportunity, and explains why people who were enthusiastic roller or ice skaters in years past find in-line skating so easy their first day. For many others, it means "practice makes perfect," because every moment of skating time is recorded in that internal gyroscope, improving your balance permanently.

While you can learn the basic stride and turns during your first skating session, you should be pretty impressed with yourself after about 20 hours on skates. This is when you start feeling more coordinated and, therefore, more confident. As you read this book, you will go out and repeat each lesson's drills until you feel ready to move on to the next one. If you're physically capable of it, try to plan on one and a half to two hours for each lesson.

How to be an "expert" beginner

To build confidence and skills quickly, take special care in selecting your learning place. Refer to "Best beginner locations" on page 27 to look for a paved area near your home, school, or job where you can go often to practice skating. The closer to home it is, the more likely you'll get in more practice time. Empty parking lots and unused ball courts are fine choices. Though desirable as a learning location, it's harder to find dis-traction-free time at indoors rinks. At all costs, avoid hills until you've mastered stopping and speed control techniques. See Chapter 8 for more location ideas.

Consider joining a skating club if one meets regularly in your community. Skating with others is one of the fastest ways to learn, because observation and emulation are great teachers. Ask about clubs at your local skate shops. And of course, inquire about the availability of lessons from an IISA-certified instructor.

The phrase "expert beginner" may sound odd, but for a skater with the right outlook it's not a contradiction. Unlike many sports that require years of practice, in-line skating is rewarding the very first day you try it. Even the basic skills are enough to provide most of the fun and fitness in-line skating has to offer.

Your mind is the only obstacle to advancing beyond the forward glide and some minimal turning skills. And once you've learned the basics, your mind is usually what's behind out-of-control crashes and careless mistakes.

It's panic that brings the illusion that the abilities you've already mastered are suddenly not available. Unfortunately, it's also the mind that leads some skaters to leave caution and protective gear behind, increasing their injury risks.

For many beginning skaters, the fear of falling is the biggest hurdle. Add self-doubt, self-consciousness in front of others, lapses in concentration, or negative thoughts, and you end up with the physical tension and rigidity that causes awkwardness and, ultimately, loss of control. This literally translates into being "frozen with fear," making you too stiff to learn the movements that can keep you safe on skates. (If this sounds like you, spend the first five minutes of every skate session on the lawn reviewing the in-line fundamentals starting on page 57.)

You can, however, reduce such tension when you take charge of the elements that affect your learning experience. The resulting sense of control will ease away most of those debilitating thoughts. Here are some factors you can influence:

Variables. When you add new skating skills, practice them at the same location where you learned them. The less variation you encounter in your learning environment, the better you can concentrate on the basics. Besides location, other distracting variables could include changes to your skate setup, a new skating companion, or gusty winds.

Repetition. Practice often. You will find that in this sport, repetition is not boring. The simple joy of movement will propel you on, whether you're at an indoor rink or in the great outdoors. Working on recently learned techniques will provide a foundation for adding more advanced ones later. If possible, skate no less than twice a week to keep your learning curve in a strong upward arc.

Observation. You can learn faster by noticing how your skates and balance react to different pressures and angles. Experiment. Analyze. Watch and try to copy other skaters. Pay special attention to how your body moves when learning turning skills to better translate these to your weaker side.

Playfulness. Many skaters take themselves beyond the basics just by getting out on the pavement for hours of play. Once you're comfortable with the rolling feeling and how to use your heel brake, you should make time to go out and fool around as often as possible.

26

Photo by Liz Miller

Music. Try to make music a part of some practice sessions. Tempos and tunes can do wonders to promote spontaneous skating; a strong rhythmic beat will inspire you to perform repetitious drills more fluidly and with less conscious effort. If you're someplace where it won't disturb others, turn up the volume on a portable radio or tape player. Headphones are too dangerous because they obstruct the sound of approaching vehicles, cyclists, and other potential dangers outside your peripheral vision.

Confidence. To dramatically boost your confidence so you can relax and learn how to skate, wear *all* of your protective gear every time you skate—that's the easy part—, and learn how stop with your heel brake as soon as possible—not quite so easy! Begin each learning session by reviewing what you have already mastered, even if that means going back to the carpet or lawn.

BEST BEGINNER LOCATIONS

As a beginner, you need skating terrain that's completely hill- and vehicle-free, smooth, and conveniently located, the closer to home the better. Explore your weekly routes with an in-line skater's perspective. You may be commuting past virtual skating Meccas without even realizing it.

Paved surfaces can vary greatly from area to area. Dark black asphalt looks inviting because it is new, but it doesn't always offer the smoothness skaters like. You can usually tell what the texture will feel like on skates by looking at it close up or by sliding the

> ### TIPS FOR SKATING IN THE WORLD
> To find new skating locations outside your region, ask the employees at a local skate, skateboard, surf, or bicycle shop.

Business parks after hours. After 6 p.m. or on weekends, business area pavement is great for exploration and practice. Often these complexes contain vast parking lots and wide sidewalks bordered by manicured lawns. There is minimum car traffic and maximum acreage, beckoning you to skate a few laps or work on mobility skills. Streets in business park complexes can be virtually deserted on weekends, and for this reason, they're often used by in-liners for workouts or speed skating events.

If you work in a business park, make a noon time (non-skating) expedition through the parking lots and streets nearby. You may be lucky enough to find vacant parking areas within safe skating distance that would be good for lunch-hour sessions.

Quiet neighborhood streets. If you live in a suburb, there may be practice terrain right outside your door. If there is a smoothly paved cul de sac or a street nearby that doesn't get much traffic, you have the perfect skating location. Such convenience can't help but speed up your learning process.

sole of your shoe lightly across the surface to test the roughness. If you still can't tell, go ahead and give it a try on skates. If your feet vibrate too much for smooth coasting, cross this site off your list for now.

Debris can make perfectly even pavement unsafe. Gravel, acorns, leaves, puddles, oil patches, and a coating of fine sand can be very slippery, leading to some pretty exciting recoveries. And beware: no matter what the location, you will find hills where you never thought there were any.

Here's a list of good beginner locations:

School yards. A neighborhood school might provide the nearest "skating rink." (Be sure no signs are posted prohibiting skating on campus.) School yards offer parking lots and play areas with painted circles where you can practice turning skills. Pavement quality can be at its finest on a volleyball or tennis court. In some cases, these are actually set aside for in-line hockey practice.

Church parking lots. If the pavement is smooth and nobody minds, these are likely to be traffic-free much of the time.

Photo by Jeff Dowling,
courtesy of Fitness & SpeedSkating Times

City parks. Some city parks have enough room for skaters to share the sidewalks with pedestrians. San Francisco's Golden Gate Park barricades certain streets on Sundays so pedestrians, cyclists and skaters can enjoy it traffic-free. Skating in a park is a great opportunity to meet other skaters. Besides making new friends, you can watch and learn from more experienced skaters, who will most likely be complimented by your interest and willing to give pointers.

In larger cities, look for an area in the park where a boom box attracts a group of skaters. Skating to music may inspire you to relax some inhibitions and try imitating the better skaters.

Bike paths. Beginners can enjoy uncrowded bike paths with no hills. However, many long bike paths come with dips and hills, or surprise patches of debris. The safest way to determine if a bike path will be suitable is to walk it or test it on a bike.

Preparing for other in-line disciplines

Once you've learned the basics of striding, turning and stopping, you can focus on learning the skills that will prepare you for participation in sports enjoyed passionately by skaters all over the world.

Roller hockey, speed skating, and aggressive skating (ramps, stunts and street), have attracted so many followers that each has its own amateur and professional competitive circuits.

Since in-line skaters have come to the sport from an ever-increasing variety of backgrounds, a mix of hybrid sports emerged by the late 1990s. Alongside roller hockey, in-line soccer and in-line basketball became popular in some metropolitan areas. Even if you don't plan to branch out from recreational skating, you will become a more well-rounded, balanced skater if you try to learn other forms of the sport.

The most popular in-line disciplines are described on the following pages, followed the skills that serve as each one's building blocks and any associated publications and organizations. If you are interested in pursuing a specific discipline, go through this book with page markers and flag the building block skills so you can make those drills a learning priority.

RECREATIONAL
Approximately 90% of the world's in-line skaters are recreational participants, skating primarily for pleasure and fitness. (We may not get much media attention, but we still rule!) As an intermediate recreational skater,

you can easily benefit from a workout that is comparable to biking, and with some practice, running. The lessons and advice in the remainder of this book are written with the recreational skater in mind.

AGGRESSIVE
Young skaters are drawn to the thrills of launching off a ramp to do aerial stunts, swooping up and down a quarter- or half-pipe, and "grinding" any curb, railing, and tree planter in sight. Besides specialized equipment and daring (or a willingness to

---

TIPS FOR SKATING IN THE WORLD
When crossing a street with oncoming traffic or tricky pavement, give yourself enough time to lurch or fall and still get across safely.

Photo by Liz Miller

run from the law), aggressive skating demands precise footwork, excellent balance, and more than a little endurance, in every sense of the word.

FITNESS

Excellent fitness benefits are within reach of experienced skaters who have access to long, uninterrupted trails or routes. Since the fluid in-line stride delivers nonimpact benefits to the cardiovascular system, body composition, and muscles, in-line workouts are ideal for those interested in building and maintaining healthy bodies through sustained physical effort regardless of age.

FREESTYLE

Freestyle includes everything from line dancing to the funky beat of a boom box to performance figure skating. Recreational skates remain the favorite footwear, especially on the street. However, there are now skates specifically designed for off-ice figure

skating, complete with leather boots and a rolling toe stop that emulates the pick used for launching into jumps or spins. Look for this discipline to grow as a result.

ROLLER HOCKEY

The first modern in-lines were invented by an avid ice hockey player searching for a way to continue training year-round. Roller hockey was already being played on conventional roller skates (now referred to as "quad" skates), but participation exploded with the advent of in-lines.

Novice skaters who start playing roller hockey report that the excitement generated by team dynamics, stick handling and competitive play add up to a shorter learning curve for all striding and maneuvering skills. Players have to think on their feet instead of about their feet. As for gear, each non-goalie player needs a hockey stick, protective gloves, a face shield and mouthpiece, hockey pants, shin guards, shoulder pads and, for males, a jock strap and cup. Goalies need even more gear, so start saving your lunch money now!

SKATE TO SKI

In 1986, the US Ski Team and the Professional Ski Instructors Association (PSIA) discovered in-lines for dry-land performance training programs to improve the team's slalom skiing technique. Skaters who cross-train with ski poles become better, more centered snow skiers. Case in point: your intrepid author.

SPEED SKATING

For competitive souls who enjoy a high-speed or long in-line workout, racing is the natural next stroke. Taking it a bit further, several ice speed skating medalists at the 2002 Winter Olympics came from an in-line background! In-line racing entered the 1990s on the urethane wheels of both ice and quad speed skating converts. It tends to cater to the elite athlete, due in part to the expense of lightweight custom boots, precision bearings, five-wheel frames and fresh wheels.

Today there are many nonprofessional short- and long-distance race events to choose from, both indoors and outdoors. Many include "fun rolls" offering interested amateurs a taste of the race. In fact, the vast majority of most in-line marathon participants are avid recreational and fitness skaters who love skating long distances.

Building Blocks for the Future

Use the information on this and the following pages to map out a custom *Get Rolling* lesson plan. You'll find a list of skill building blocks for each of the various skate disciplines along with the associated page numbers in this book. I have also provided the latest information on related resources (web sites, books, organizations) to help you find out more about each discipline.

Recreational Building Blocks
- Beginning Skills chapter (p. 57)
- Intermediate Skills chapter (p. 85)

Resources:

- International Inline Skating Association (IISA); www.iisa.org/index.htm

- International Inline Skating Association's Inline Skating Laws and Advocacy advice page; www.iisa.org/legal/

- USA Roller Sports Fitness Skating Club; www.usarollersports.com/fitness/fitnessclubs.htm

- USA Roller Sports Magazine; www.usarollersports.com/publications/

- National Skate Patrol (NSP); www.iisa.org/nsp

- GetRolling.com (help for beginners); www.getrolling.com

- CASkating.com (California trails database); www.caskating.com

- SkateGRRL.com (online directory); www.skategrrl.com

Aggressive Building Blocks
- Lunge Turn (p. 91)
- T-Stop (p. 101)
- One-Footed Glides (p. 82)
- 180-degree Transitions (p. 98)
- Hop-Overs (p. 110)

Resources:
- *Daily Bread* (magazine); www.dbmag.com
- Aggressive Skaters Association; www.asaskate.com
- Skatepark Association of the USA; www.spausa.org
- *Advanced Inline Skating*, by Liz Miller (book); www.getrolling.com

Fitness Building Blocks
- Power Stride (p. 95)
- Forward Crossovers (p. 85)
- Forward Swizzle (p. 75)
- Backward Swizzle (p. 89)
- Half Swizzles (p. 93)

Resources:
- *Fitness and Speedskating Times* (magazine); www.fasst.com
- Rails-to-Trails Conservancy; www.railtrails.org
- Intermodal Surface Transportation Efficiency Act (ISTEA); www.tea3.org/about.asp
- *Advanced Inline Skating*, by Liz Miller (book); www.getrolling.com
- *Fitness Inline Skating*, by Suzanne Nottingham and Frank Fedel; (book) www.amazon.com

- *Skate Fit: the Complete In-Line Skating Workout,* by Carolyn Bradley (video) www.amazon.com

Freestyle Building Blocks
- Backward Skating (p. 88)
- T-Stops (p. 101)
- Backward Crossovers (p. 107)
- Single-Foot Glide (p. 82)
- Hop-Overs (p. 110)
- 180-degree Transitions (p. 98)

Resources:
- International Inline Figure Skating Association; www.iifsa.com
- USA Roller Sports (USARS); www.usarollersports.org
- USA Roller Sports Magazine; www.usarollersports.com/publications
- *How to Jump and Spin on Inline Skates,* by Jo Ann Schneider Farris (book); www.1stbooks.com
- *Advanced Inline Skating*, by Liz Miller (book); www.getrolling.com
- *Rollerdance,* by Richard Humphrey; (videos) http://www.rollerdance.com/

Hockey Building Blocks
- 180-degree Transitions (p. 98)
- Forward Crossovers (p. 85)
- Backward Crossovers (p. 107)
- Backward Power Slide (p. 103)
- Backward Skating (p. 88)
- Lunge Stop (p. 104)
- Lunge Turn (p. 91)
- Parallel Turn (p. 78)
- T-Stops (p. 101)

Resources:

- Roller Hockey Magazine; www.rhockey.com
- USA Roller Sports (USARS); www.usarollersports.org
- USA Roller Sports Magazine; www.usarollersports.com/publications
- *Advanced Inline Skating*, by Liz Miller (book); www.getrolling.com

Skate-to-Ski Building Blocks

- Beginning (p. 57) and Intermediate Skills (p. 85) chapters
- Advanced Slaloms chapter (p. 115)
- Parallel Turn (p. 78)
- Slalom Turn (p. 94)

Resources:

- International Inline Downhill Association (IIDA); www.inlinedownhill.com
- International Gravity Sports Association (IGSA); www.gravity-sports.com
- *Advanced Inline Skating*, by Liz Miller (book); www.getrolling.com

Speed Skating Building Blocks

- Power Stride (p. 95)
- Forward Swizzle (p. 75)
- Forward Crossovers (p. 85)
- T-Stops (p. 101)
- Lunge Turn (p. 91)
- Snow Plow (p. 105)

Resources:

- Fitness and Speedskating Times (magazine); www.fasst.com
- World Inline Speed Skaters Association; www.nrpatin.org.co/wisa_home.htm
- USA Roller Sports (USARS); www.usarollersports.org
- USA Roller Sports Magazine; www.usarollersports.com/publications
- *Speed on Skates*, by Barry Publow (book); www.breakawayskate.com
- *Advanced Inline Skating*, by Liz Miller (book); www.getrolling.com

CHAPTER 2

Avoiding Injury

It would be inappropriate and wrong for me to suggest that you won't ever fall down or experience the occasional bruise or scrape during your skating lifetime. Situations beyond your control will arise from time to time due to surprises in your skating environment or temporary lapses of attention. That's the way the world is.

But because 99% of in-line safety is a matter of choice, the likelihood of a serious injury on in-line skates is largely within your control. By embracing every available safety option, you can attain your maximum abilities without fear of major trauma.

You choose how safe you will be by wearing protective gear, learning the basic skills, adopting an expert's attitude, staying in shape, and practicing good skate maintenance. That's what this chapter is about.

Protective gear

The vast majority of in-line injuries can be prevented by wearing the protective gear. The Consumer Product Safety Commission recommends that, at minimum, everyone should wear a helmet and wrist guards on every skating venture. Those items, plus knee and elbow pads, are musts for emergency stopping maneuvers, hills, and such aggressive moves as ramp skating and riding stairs. The baggy shorts you see on stunt

skaters often conceal hip and tailbone protection. Street hockey should be played with all available safety gear; it doesn't take long to find out why.

More often than not, the skaters least likely to wear protective gear have the greatest tendency to engage in high-risk behavior. "Too cool" to wear full protection, they're often far too willing to take on hills, stairs, traffic, and other challenges before they're ready. Though people in this category may go on to become tomorrow's roller-hockey stars or Olympic freestylers, they contribute the most to today's in-line injury statistics.

According to a year-long study by the Centers for Disease Control and Prevention (CDC) using the National Electronic Injury Surveillance System, males were injured 30 percent more than females while skating; for teens, the injury ratio leaped to 90 percent more males than females (almost two boys injured for every girl).

Don't go to a toy or discount store to buy your helmet and pads. The quality of mass-market protective gear is horrendous. Sporting goods stores that sell in-lines all carry a variety of well-made gear. Sometimes protective pads come prepackaged as a set, but beware, some combo packs don't include all three pieces. They vary in price by a few dollars a pair, so it doesn't hurt to comparison-shop while you're pricing skates. Detailed advice on buying helmets and protective pads appears in Chapter 3, Getting Equipped.

HELMETS

Helmets play a powerful role in preventing head injuries, which can be the most deadly. Statistics reveal that in-line skating beginners are at a greater risk for injuries to the back of the head because their early strokes are straight-legged, resulting in a tendency to fall backward. But helmets don't become optional later on. Experienced skaters push their limits over time, *increasing* the need for protection as they become better skaters.

Unfortunately, most skaters do not wear helmets, although many have heard horror stories about deadly head injuries. It usually takes a brush with death to convince people that a helmet is absolutely essential gear.

Besides the obvious safety benefits, there are other reasons to slap on a brain bucket: to set a good example for friends (and, especially, kids); to improve your ability to compete hard without injury (as do hockey players, freestylers, and speed skaters: definitely not geeks); and best of all, to gain more confidence while learning new skills.

Finally, a helmet makes you more noticeable to motorists, who might otherwise expect you to behave like a pedestrian, at pedestrian speeds. Put a cell-phone in the driver's hands, and helmetless you could be the victim of a tragic lack of attention!

Wear your helmet correctly (see the diagram in "Adjusting the Helmet Fit" on page 53). Adjust the chin straps so it fits snugly, covers your forehead, and doesn't shift from front to back or side to side. If your forehead is exposed, your brain is, too, and that's not much better than skating helmetless.

Don't wait for your own or a loved one's brush with death to be convinced, okay?

WRIST GUARDS

Emergency room studies completed from 1992 to 1994 by Dr. Richard Schieber at the Centers for Disease Control and Prevention showed that skaters who do not wear wrist guards increase their risk of injury by 1,000 percent! Even the most skilled or cautious skaters can be tripped up by other skaters, cyclists, or pavement debris. Your hands are your first instinctive defense for preventing a head injury during a fall: so make sure you protect them by wearing wrist guards.

If you're reluctant, just imagine how life would be if you were unable to feed and clothe yourself, write, use your computer, or drive, even for a short time. With one or both wrists immobilized in a cast or bandages, you'd be dependent on others to perform the most basic daily tasks. Worse, you might be unable to work, meaning no income for skating vacations!

KNEE AND ELBOW PADS

Protective pads designed for use on streets and trails have a slick surface so they will slide easily across the pavement, deflecting some of the impact that could injure your joints. Later in this book you will learn how to use your gear to make a controlled fall.

Though they don't mean the difference between life and death, knee and elbow pads are good protection for beginners and experts alike. Wrists and knees are both likely to hit the ground when you fall. Elbow pads are the least used item by the general skating community, but they're valuable protection for your boniest joints, especially for stunt practice and the high speeds of downhill skating. But even something as mundane as a hard swerve to avoid a child on a tricycle can cause a sideways, bone-shattering fall.

Qualified instruction

You'll dramatically lower your risk of injury if you master all skating basics before exploring the local pavement. Instruction can vary from the quick freebie when you rent, to store-sponsored lessons, to classes offered by a certified in-line instructor.

However you start out, you can keep learning at your own pace with an instructional video or book such as this one. While books abound, there are very few decent videos available. Your best resource for the latest and greatest is to search the World Wide Web for "inline skating videos."

A safe learning location is also crucial. (See "Best beginner locations" on page 27.) Ideally, the first few moments on skates should be spent on carpeting or dry grass. From there, a park with wide, flat sidewalks bordered by grass is best—until you've learned how to stride, turn and stop.

To find out more about the benefits of certified instruction or to search for an instructor who teaches near you, visit the web site of the International In-Line Skating Association's Inline Certification Program at http://www.iisa.org/.

TIPS FOR SKATING IN THE WORLD
Knowing the rules of the trail when skating isn't just courtesy, it's a way to prevent serious accidents.

The expert's attitude

Because humans—and especially skaters—are free spirits, attitude is the most difficult injury factor to control. The Rules of the Road define standard behavior that covers skater safety and etiquette. Taking it a bit further, learn to appreciate how external factors such as terrain, group dynamics, and the weather also greatly affect your safety.

RULES OF THE ROAD

There are several versions of the skating code of conduct. No matter what the source, though, they all have the same goal: to teach essential trail etiquette and safety habits. The following list is distributed by the International Inline Skating Association and taught by its certified instructors.

Skate Smart
- Always wear your helmet, wrist guards, knee, and elbow pads.
- Learn the basics: speed control, turning, braking, and stopping.
- Keep all of your equipment in safe condition (see the Skate Maintenance section later in this chapter).

Skate Legal
- Observe all traffic regulations; on skates, you must obey vehicle laws.
- Skate with, not against the flow of traffic.
- Don't "skitch"—never allow yourself to be towed by a vehicle or bicycle.

Skate Alert
- Always skate in control.

- Stay away from water, oil, debris, sand, and uneven or broken pavement.
- Avoid areas with heavy traffic.
- Avoid wearing headphones or anything that makes it hard to hear.

Skate Polite
- Skate on the right side of the path and call out a warning before you pass on the left ("Passing your left!").
- Yield to pedestrians.
- Stop stroking in order to make room for passing cyclists (and avoid catching a skate in their spokes!).
- Be a good-will ambassador for in-line skating.

KNOW THE TERRAIN AND CONDITIONS
Take care to choose a route you can handle. Before skating on a new or steeply sloped trail, make sure you are able to:

- negotiate sudden encounters with speed bumps, garden hoses, curbs, rough patches, or gravel;
- slow down and come to a full stop for intersections;
- stop abruptly or swerve to avoid sudden obstacles;
- make an emergency exit from a slope onto the road's shoulder;

TIPS FOR SKATING IN THE WORLD
Learn early how to coast with your brake foot scissored forward 6 to 8 inches. That makes a longer base to handle the lurching caused by rough patches or cracks.

- ride your heel brake, drag one skate in a T-Stop position, or make Slalom Turns to reduce speed; and
- remain in control if a car tailgates you and honks.

Trail conditions can change unexpectedly, even in a single day. Save your skating trip for some other time if:

- it is foggy or dark outside, or if a rainstorm is brewing;
- you (or drivers in oncoming traffic) will be heading directly into the sun;
- the trail surface is slick due to recent rain, fog, wet leaves, or sprinklers.

SKATING ALONE
Generally, you can feel safe skating solo in the daytime. Stay alert when passing through run-down urban neighborhoods or road underpasses. Use caution and common sense. If the trail seems to attract loiterers, for instance, or you see lots beer or liquor bottles or graffiti, take these as signs you should not be skating here after sunset. When daylight is waning, don't fool around; skate hard and fast and get a good workout on the way back to your car.

Women in particular should observe certain security measures. Skate with a friend when possible. Never acknowledge or respond to harassing remarks, gestures, or sounds from male strangers, including school-age boys. Be wary of male pedestrians; acknowledge their presence with a short passing glance, but don't smile or sustain eye contact. Don't appear unsure of where you are going. When you look the picture of confidence and skate with authority, you're less likely to be hassled.

GROUP CONDUCT

How you skate in a group can greatly affect your safety. When skating with others, keep the following pointers in mind:

- Keep plenty of distance from other skaters so you have enough room to respond to their maneuvers.

- Look out for each other by calling out warnings about cars or obstacles on the trail.

- Resist peer pressure to skate beyond your own control and comfort zones.

- Have an experienced skater bring up the rear to assist any stragglers.

PREPARING FOR THE ELEMENTS

As long as the pavement is dry, you can skate outdoors no matter what the weather. When it comes to environmental factors, oily, wet or icy pavement are the only conditions you need to worry about because they're slick or may get your bearings wet. If you can't avoid such surfaces, stop stroking. Approach with enough speed to be able to coast across, or take very short, light-pressure strokes to reach the other side. See "Stride One (the beginning stride)" on page 64.

Cold weather alone should not keep you off your wheels. Because in-line skating is such great overall exercise, you can build up body warmth within a few minutes. The trick is to prepare for it in the same way joggers or cross-country skiers do. Dress in multiple light layers. Depending on the temperature, you may want to wear thermal tights that wick moisture away from your skin, a turtleneck, a windbreaker, and thermal head and hand coverings under your helmet and gloves. If the wind is blowing enough to make your eyes water, a pair of close-fitting goggle-style sunglasses (like Panoptx) may help. Wear a daypack or sports fanny pack that's roomy enough to store any removed layers. You'll soon learn how much to wear as you try skating on frosty mornings or chilly afternoons.

Of course, bright, sunny days are the most enticing. In the sun, make sure you add one more protective layer besides your safety gear, a high SPF sunscreen. Sunglasses and a visor that fits under your helmet are also good to have.

On extremely hot days, take every precaution against dehydration. If you don't own a hydration pack, drink lots of liquid before you go out. Pack two bottles of water, one in your daypack or fanny pack, and the other awaiting your return (in a cooler if necessary) in your car. Once you start enjoying yourself, it's easy to forget you are perspiring away your body's store of water.

TIPS FOR SKATING IN THE WORLD

When skating behind a partner down a long hill, leave plenty of room so you have enough time to react safely to his or her unexpected actions or a fall.

You may not want to skate when it's blustery, but wind can actually enhance your trip, especially if you're interested in a workout. Skating against the wind lets you build extra stroking power while working on sprints or speed skating skills. And when the wind is at your back, the boost makes flat pavement feel like downhill, a situation just right for practicing easy slalom-skating turns. Try to skate into the breeze at the beginning of your trip when you're most energetic; fighting wind resistance all the way back to the car can be brutal when you're tired.

Physical fitness

Your risk of injuries will be far lower if you have an exercise habit that's at least six months old. Teaching skaters of all ages and backgrounds has proved to me that it is possible for a person to be in poor physical condition without any appearance of being flabby.

Plain and simple, people who have a regular, moderate fitness program are more durable, coordinated, and balanced their first day of skating, and usually pop right up off the pavement when they do fall.

On the other hand, even if they look fit on the outside, people with a sedentary lifestyle have low muscle mass along with weak tendons and ligaments. That makes them frighteningly "floppy" as beginning skaters, because they fall lots more than fit people and are more easily injured by the impact. A little bit of muscle tone would contribute greatly towards a more stable start.

> **TIPS FOR SKATING IN THE WORLD**
> Remove your sunglasses just before entering a dark underpass or tunnel to better see any debris or sand that may lurk there. Consider closing an eye several yards before entering so at least one eye is prepared for the dark.

But floppy people, don't despair! See "Yoga for Skaters" on page 137. This Appendix shows how the ancient practice of Yoga can get you fit for the modern sport of skating by increasing your balance, strength and flexibility both on and off skates—and so much more!

Skate maintenance

If you follow the advice offered in the Getting Equipped chapter (starting on page 47) and purchase a decent pair of in-lines, you're halfway to optimum skate safety. After that, don't just take it for granted they'll remain in pristine condition forever. Pay attention to the wear on permanent and replaceable components. A sudden buckle, wheel or boot failure can slap you down and lead to painful consequences.

Take good care of your in-line skates, and the investment will pay dividends for years. You can prevent some wear by storing them properly and keeping them clean. It's easy to replace the brake pad. Periodically rotating your wheels and cleaning your bearings aren't quite so easy, but since these parts are relatively expensive to replace, it's a money-saving step that's worth the hassle.

AFTER EVERY SKATE

Preventive maintenance is as simple as a quick hardware check and properly storing your boots after each excursion.

Examine your skates when you take them off to make sure the wheels and bearings are dry, and nothing is caught in the frame.

The boot liners will be warm and moist when you step out of them, and the tongue can easily dry out in an unnatural shape. To prevent crimped sides that will bite into your foot, carefully arrange the tongue in its proper position, then buckle or lace the boot closed to keep it there. Really soaked liners, however, should be removed from the boots to dry. For long-term storage (for example, during winter), buckle the liners inside the boots as described above and store them in a dry and dust-free location.

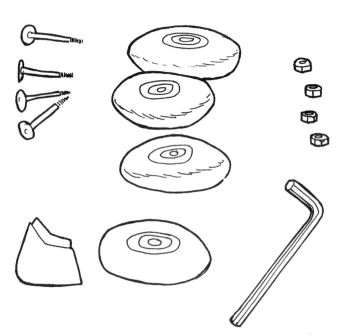

REPLACING THE HEEL BRAKE

When your brake pad is worn to half an inch, you need to

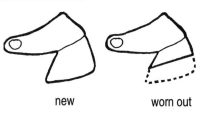

new   worn out

replace it. On most skates, this is a simple matter of unbolting it from the wheel frame and inserting a new brake pad. Sometimes, you must also remove the rear wheel.

ROTATING THE WHEELS

Because most activity on skates originates from a push against the inside wheel edges, these begin to wear off and flatten, a condition skaters call "coned." Regularly rotating and flipping the wheels over extends wheel life considerably.

Get yourself organized before you disassemble your skates. Make sure you have enough room to lay out a soft rag, an old toothbrush, the wrench(es) that came packaged with your skates, and your removed wheels and bolts.

1. Take the skate with the brake and grip it upside down between your thighs, toe end facing out.

2. Using the wrenches, remove all four wheels and set them aside in a line that matches their positions in the frame.

3. Dampen and use the cloth to wipe down the surface of your boot, including inside the wheel frame.

4. Wipe down each removed wheel and lightly brush the grit off the bearing on both sides with the toothbrush.

5. Make sure the frame is completely dry before reinstalling the wheels and brake.

6. In rotating the wheel positions, take these steps to extend their life:

   • Refer to the diagram below or swap the most worn wheels (usually toe and heel) with the least worn ones.

   • Flip the wheels over so the shaved-off edges face the outside of the foot on each boot.

   • If one set of wheels is a lot more worn than the other, swap the right skate's wheels with the left.

recreational skate

fitness or speed skate

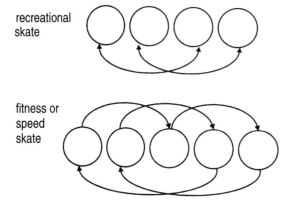

TIPS FOR SKATING IN THE WORLD
Make sure your heel brake is fresh before starting a long trip where you'll be skating on steep, rough surfaces, or across many intersections.

7. Tighten each bolt so it feels snug. Then spin the wheel to make sure there is no undue resistance.

REPLACING THE WHEELS

Elite speed skaters will replace wheels the moment the original racing profile is worn off. This would be very expensive except for the fact that these athletes are often sponsored by manufacturers.

As a recreational skater, you will be more likely to need replacements a couple of times a year, depending on how hard and often you skate. Wheel wear depends on the quantity and style of skating you enjoy and whether you skate on soft wheels (which wear out faster) or hard wheels.

Replace your wheels when the markings on the wheel sidewalls are worn off or if rotating no longer fixes the sawed-off look. Regular rotating ensures that all of the wheels will need replacing at the same time.

worn out   new

When replacing your wheels, you (or your shop) must remove your bearings from the old wheels and install them in the new ones. Beware, do-it-yourselfers: it's very easy to damage the bearing shield when trying to push bearings out of a wheel without the proper tools! The voice of experience...

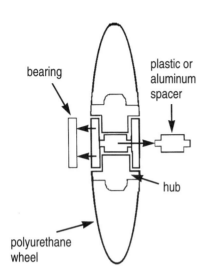

bearing

plastic or aluminum spacer

hub

polyurethane wheel

First, remove all wheels and wipe off loose dirt. Lightly brush off the surface of the bearings with a toothbrush. Then, for each wheel:

1. Grasping the wheel in one hand, use a bearing pusher to push the spacer in the center of the bearing out the other side, with the bearing ahead of it.

2. Flip the wheel over and push out the second bearing.

3. Pick up a new wheel and press in a bearing. Flip the wheel and insert the spacer, followed by the second bearing. Reinstall the wheels and you're set to go.

ROCKERING THE WHEELS

Some in-line skates allow you to drop the center wheels a fraction of an inch (called rockering) so that the wheel base arcs slightly, enabling tighter turns. The trade-off is that this reduces the skate's stability for general recreational skating or for skating fast and straight. If your skates allow rockering, the holes in the axle guides will be offset from the center or your wheel bolts will have two installation positions.

Warning: If your wheels are badly worn, rockering will feel very unstable. Postpone your first rockering experiment until the next time you replace your wheels. The following instructions apply to skates with removable axel guides.

1. Remove your skates' center wheels to expose the axle guides that are typically embedded into both screw holes on the sides of the wheel frame.

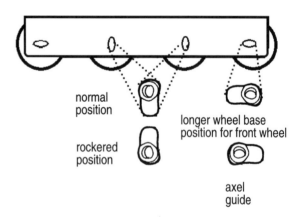

normal position

rockered position

longer wheel base position for front wheel

axel guide

2. Pull out each axle guide, rotate it to the rockered position, and push it back into the side of the frame.

3. Reinstall the wheels.

If your skates can be rockered using the wheel bolts, they will have a flat side or an etched arrow to indicate installation options.

LENGTHENING THE WHEEL BASE

Some in-line skate frames are set up so you can move the front and rear wheels farther apart on the frame, resulting in a longer wheel base. This longer spread improves stability for recreational or speed skating. (By contrast, a shorter wheel base complements rockered wheels.) If your skates allow this adjustment, the holes in the axle guides will be offset from the center. (See illustration on previous page.)

1. Remove the front and rear wheels of the skate to expose the plastic guides embedded into both screw holes on the sides of the wheel frame.

2. Pull out each axle guide, rotate it to the lengthened position, and push it back into the side of the frame.

3. Reinstall the wheels.

CLEANING THE BEARINGS

For the recreational skater, one set of bearings should last through at least five or more wheel changes. You can put off replacement and avoid frequent bearing maintenance if you stay away from puddles, sand, and fine gravel. Technically, skating through some sand or water shouldn't do damage if you give your equipment immediate apres-skate attention, but since we humans have a natural tendency to procrastinate, avoiding those conditions is the best protection. Otherwise, you will find that you're skating more slowly with more effort, or you'll hear that telltale squeak of sand in your bearings.

Recreational skaters don't need to be concerned with interior bearing maintenance unless the mechanics of the process are just too fascinating to resist. Instructions for these procedures are beyond the scope of this book but are well covered on the World Wide Web. Bearing maintenance can be also be learned by making friends with an employee at your local skate shop.

You can upgrade to high-performance bearings that are designed for self-maintenance. Their removable shields allow you to easily disassemble and soak them in a solvent that dislodges grit. Standard sealed wheel bearings can be converted for regular clean-and-lubes by removing one shield. This step is non-reversible but as long as the exposed side of the bearing faces inside, it'll stay clean. You can use a tiny, sharp object (such as an eyeglass screwdriver) to pry off one shield, or you can have the conversion done at your local skate shop.

TIPS FOR SKATING IN THE WORLD

Keep your bearings clean and dry and they'll last for years. For recreational skaters it's just not necessary to spend hours on bearing cleaning or money on replacements more often than every 4-5 years.

Avoiding Injury

CHAPTER 3

Getting Equipped

Pick your skate store carefully, and it could be the start of a long and beneficial relationship. A shop's special services may be more important than its price tags. Sometimes, a skate purchase includes free maintenance or discounts on replacement parts.

A skate shop is your best source of information about local lessons, clubs, race programs, hockey teams, or good locations.

Skate specialty stores may be hard to find since the boom of the mid-nineties has waned. The most likely retailers today are ski, bike or skateboard shops. Sporting goods chains and department stores may sell skates, but won't offer any amenities and rarely have informed staff.

A good skate store will have staff who can help you with the best boot fit and explain the differences among skate models, wheels and bearings. If the skate you want is not in stock or not part of the standard inventory, some shops will special-order them. Once you find such a store, be sure to check out their stock of skating accessories and replacement brakes and check to see if they carry any videos or books.

Skates are not toys

Before you begin trying on skates, be sure to read the first part of the Beginning Skills chapter (page 57), which covers how to rise safely from a chair or bench, how to stand still using the Safe-T position, and how to make those first tentative moves.

RENTALS

If you're unsure about adding in-line skating as a new activity, see if you can rent a pair first. Unfortunately, with the passing of the boom, in-line skate rentals may be even harder to find than skate specialty shops. If your local ski, bike or skateboard shops don't pan out, try looking at the listings under "Skating" in the yellow pages. Be sure your rental skates come with a heel brake and that all protective gear is provided, including a helmet.

Ask if the rental fee can be applied towards the purchase of your own new pair of in-lines. If you don't mind starting with used skates and you like the ones you rented, ask when the rental line will go on sale. You can find some great deals in the rental bins in late summer.

Once you're rolling, it may take an hour or so before any feature of a skate boot starts to bother you. If at all possible, try renting different models, either on the same day or over several days.

DON'T BE A CHEAPSKATE

Too often, the main priority of first-time buyers is to spend as little money as possible, which invariably leads to a disappointing introduction to the sport. Low-end skates are built of low-quality materials, usually resulting in foot pain, poor stability, sluggish bearings and a rough ride. Cheap skates are more likely to break, too. Broken buckles or detached wheels can be dangerous when they occur at a roll.

Unlike higher-quality skates, cheaper models often can't be upgraded with new brakes, better wheels, or faster bearings. Their unwitting new owners, discouraged when they just can't seem to keep up with other skaters or manage the basics, think it's their own lack of skill that's the problem. Those who persevere end up spending more money on upgrades or on new, better-quality skates.

Here are some practical tips for purchasing in-line skates for yourself or for kids:

- In-line skates are not toys and should not be purchased at a toy store. Go to a skate retailer or sporting-goods store where you can find a wider selection and qualified sales staff to answer your questions and make suggestions.

- Invest as much as you can afford. For adults, a pair of skates that retails for less than $180 will cost more money than a better pair in the long run. Sometimes an extra $10 determines whether or not you will be able to upgrade a skate's components later on.

- Buy skates on sale. Manufacturers put out a new line of skates every year, and last year's models are almost always at least 40% off.

- If you're outfitting a child, purchase a model of skate that has an expandable wheel base or comes with two boot liners, allowing it to accommodate four full sizes. These are made by the top manufacturers and retail for about $75. Sizes start at one for most kids' models, which means even a child just out of the toddler stage can learn how to skate if motivated enough.

- Novices need a skate with superior ankle support. Look for a high, molded-plastic cuff and at least one buckle at the top. Unless you're sure you'll be moving on to play in-line hockey, don't start out with laces-only skates, which tend to loosen up and lead to wobbly ankles.

- Check with sales staff to make sure replacement wheels and brakes are available for the skate you choose.

- When trying on skates, wear a pair of absorbent socks you plan to skate in, but not too thick. Socks manufactured specifically for athletic activity are best because they are designed to "wick" the sweat away from your foot and prevent blisters.

- Consider purchasing a Rollerblade brand skate with the award-winning cuff-activated braking technology (ABT). This feature is a godsend to the sport because beginners aren't required to balance on one foot in order to learn how to stop: all eight wheels remain on the ground.

- Don't start out with five-wheel skates. They are much more expensive, more difficult to turn, and built for speed.

- Women's skate models are available from the better manufacturers. They usually compensate for the lower position of a woman's calf muscle and her narrower Achilles tendon. If the tag doesn't differentiate genders, the skate is unisex.

- Shop around. Make it a point to visit a couple of stores or call around to compare selling prices for the skates you like. With a bit of legwork, you can make sure you're getting the best deal.

RECREATIONAL SKATE FEATURES

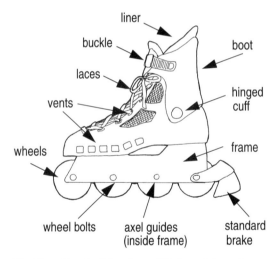

Cuff-activated brakes: It's hard to relax and enjoy liberated in-lining until you're sure of your ability to stop. The introduction of cuff-activated braking technology in 1994 made stopping much easier for beginners, letting them tackle other basic skills with more confidence. These brakes use an arm-like mechanism mounted on the back of one skate's cuff. As the cuff flexes backward in response to pressure from your calf, it forces the brake downward until it begins to drag on the pavement. (See an early model of the ABT brake in the photo on page 113.)

Don't let friends or shop personnel talk you out of purchasing a skate model with this wonderful beginner's asset! Contrary to what some well-intentioned advisors say (most of whom have never learned how to make any kind of heel brake work), cuff-activated brakes are effective and useful for all skill levels. Because the brake pad can be lowered as it wears down or raised as your braking skills improve, it's also appreciated by more experienced skaters. Finally, slalom enthusiasts can easily engage cuff-activated brakes for mid-carve speed control without interrupting their rhythm when skating downhill.

Soft vs. plastic: In the interests of lightweight breathability and comfort, most manufacturers have moved to a suede-and-mesh combination boot. In some models, the snug but cushy fit may mean slightly less support (though most are equipped with an exterior plastic cuff). Soft boot skates stay more comfortable during long skate sessions than hard plastic ones do.

Vents: Look for vents in the boot and liners in both plastic and soft boot skates. Breathability slows down the buildup of perspiration as your feet heat up. Vents improve airflow and help reduce the weight, too. Being lightweight makes any skate more maneuverable and less tiring over long periods.

Hinged cuffs: Hinged cuffs improve a skate's ankle support, forward flexibility, and stability. Many soft boot models are outfitted with a plastic hinged cuff for added support. Some forward flex stiffness is good; too much flexibility gives recreational and novice skaters less ankle support and control.

Buckles: A top buckle delivers solid ankle support. All-buckle models (plastic skates only) are easier to get on and off your feet. Laces allow the close custom fit required by speed skaters or a game of fast-action in-line hockey.

Liners: The foam-padded liners inside plastic in-line boots are replaceable, but hard to find and overpriced. In some cases, they can be removed for washing.

Sizing: Men's, women's, and junior models are usually available in a good manufacturer's skate line. Some women may find a great fit in a small men's boot (using either the men's or women's boot liner), and men with narrow feet have been known to fit comfortably into women's skates. For more sizing advice, see "How in-line skates should feel" on page 52.

Insoles: Most good-quality skates feature a removable pre-formed arch support. In some models, these may come with customizing attachments. Serious skaters insert their own arch supports or orthotic devices to fine-tune the boot's fit for maximum responsiveness.

Frames: Wheel frames accommodating three wheels are designed for smaller feet, four-wheel frames are best for recreational, hockey, and artistic skating, and five wheelers are built for stability at high speeds and powerful strides. At the specialty end, frames can be equipped with "grind plates" to facilitate rail and curb grinding, or made from strong, light weight composites for speed skaters.

Wheels: A new skate's wheels feature the diameter, core type, profile, and hardness deemed to be best suited to the features of the skate on which they are mounted. For such a small product, there is a relatively large amount of terminology, technology and hype to digest before you can become an informed buyer. Before you buy new wheels, be sure you know the maximum wheel size your skate's frames can accommodate (found in the owner's manual).

- Large-**diameter** wheels deliver the best speed for your stroke once you get going, and smaller wheels allow you to turn and accelerate more quickly. Standard wheel diameters are: 60mm for children's skates, 72mm for hockey and entry level recreational skates, 78mm for fitness, and 80mm for racing. The size is usually printed on the side of the wheel.

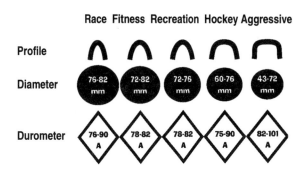

- The **profile** is the shape you see as you look at the wheel's edge. Race wheels have the narrowest profile to reduce friction from drag where the wheel touches the road. Recreation and fitness wheels have slightly wider profiles to deliver good grip during fast travel on a variety of pavement surfaces. Hockey wheels are still wider to ensure stability and quick-turning maneuverability. The fattest wheels are used by aggressive skaters for the utmost stability when performing stunts.

- Hardness, measured by a **durometer** rating, dictates a wheel's shock absorption and grip qualities, and is designated by a two-digit number followed by the letter "A." In-line wheel durometers range from a soft 74 A to a solid 101 A, (also printed on the side of the wheel). Although softer wheels grip better and reduce vibrations, they also wear out faster than harder ones.

- The core (also known as the hub) is a hard substance that the wheel's urethane bonds to, providing torsional stability and a solid seat for the bearings. Vented cores keep bearings cooler at high speeds. Smaller aggressive-style wheels have no core at all or it may be hidden inside to provide better impact handling.

To sum it up with a very specific, recreational example: if your favorite skating endeavor is fast outdoors touring on a variety of pitches and paved surfaces, then you should buy a fitness-profiled 76-78mm wheel for speed, with a 78 A durometer rating to soften the vibrations from rough asphalt.

HOW IN-LINE SKATES SHOULD FEEL

All feet are not created equal. Buying skates is like buying ski boots. They may seem comfortable to stand in, but an hour of vigorous activity may lead to the painful realization that the shell of that particular boot was not designed for your particular foot.

When checking for fit, try to keep the skates on at least 15 minutes to give them a chance to hurt. Run through the following checklist of good fit requirements. You should be satisfied in every area.

- The boot tongue is not digging into your shin or calf.

- There is no pressure on the widest part of your foot due to a narrow fit.

- There is no crease-type pressure across the tops of the toes when you flex your knees to sink lower.

- There is no specific pressure point across the top of the arch of either foot.

- Your foot is comfortably supported when you tip the skates sideways.

- The overall fit is very snug, but you can wiggle your toes.

- With straight knees, your toes lightly touch the end of the boot.

- When you bend your knees and press your shin into the tongue (this is the normal skating stance), your toes are not touching the end of the boot and your heel does not slide up and away from the sole.

Shopping for a helmet

Your helmet is the most important piece of protective gear, because, obviously, if you crack open your skull, it doesn't much matter what happens to your wrists, elbows, or knees. Here are some tips to keep in mind when choosing a helmet:

- Helmets with the ANSI or SNELL sticker of approval meet accepted impact safety standards. The N-94 standard adds an additional rating that withstands multiple (vs. single) impacts. This rating allows manufacturers designing to that standard to recommend their helmets as better protection for aggressive skating (imagine bouncing down a flight of stairs with your head).

- Different competitive skating modes call for different helmet styles; for example, ramp skaters need more overall head coverage, while speed skaters look for a more aerodynamic shape. Decide what you want to do on your skates and then ask a salesperson for guidance.

- Choose a style of helmet that is comfy and cool. For the recreational skater, vented models are lightweight and allow a cooling air flow. Bike helmets are fine.

- Shop for a close fit. If your final choice is slightly loose, make sure there's lots of extra padding strips to customize it for your head. Some helmets have an inflatable inner fit system. Padding should be sufficient to ensure the helmet doesn't shift from front to back or side to side.

ADJUSTING THE HELMET FIT

For the best protection, don't rush when adjusting the straps to fine tune your helmet's fit. You will probably need to shift the straps where they are threaded through the helmet so they intersect on both sides just below the ear lobes.

Refer to the drawing below for fitting guidelines. Allow no more than a two-fingers-sized gap under the chin. Tighten the chin strap so the helmet covers your forehead (that's where your brains are, remember!) and will remain there during vigorous activity: it should not slip to the back of your head.

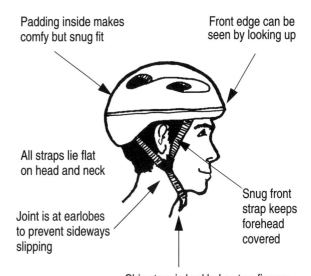

Padding inside makes comfy but snug fit

Front edge can be seen by looking up

All straps lie flat on head and neck

Joint is at earlobes to prevent sideways slipping

Snug front strap keeps forehead covered

Chin strap is buckled so two fingers can fit and/or is loose enough to allow a big yawn

Be sure to replace your helmet after it suffers a blow. Because that is likely to ruin its protective structure, some manufacturers offer a free replacement. Sun can age an exposed styrofoam helmet and reduce its effectiveness after about five years of use.

Protective pads

Beware of cheap, pre-packaged sets of protective gear. Many are too thin to adequately cushion an adult's fall. Check to make sure it's not just a set of knee and elbow pads with no wrist guards.

At some skate specialty shops you can try on padded gear specifically designed for the in-line discipline that interests you most. For example, thick pads with cloth coverings can be found for aggressive skaters who skate on slick ramps; likewise, more lightweight designs, breathable materials and reflective tape appeal to fitness skaters.

WRIST GUARDS

Wrist guards offer abrasion protection for your palms, but more important, the standard recreational wrist guard has plastic inserts on both sides of the wrist to prevent the wrist from hyper extending during crash landings.

To stay cool, find a design with breathable material on the sides. If you're willing to pay a bit more, look for wrist guards that come equipped with a rear view mirror, or articulated hinges to improve wrist movement.

KNEE PADS

Find a thick, sturdy knee pad that would protect you if you landed on it with your entire body weight. The more you fall in love with skating, the more likely this is to happen, because you'll be skating a lot. Good protection means you're more likely to skate away from a fall totally unharmed. Try the pad on if possible.

> **TIPS FOR SKATING IN THE WORLD**
> Stinky pads? You can wash most protective pads in the gentle cycle of your washing machine. They will smell much sweeter after drying in the sun.

Slip-on style knee pads are less convenient because you will have to remember to put them on before you don your skates. However, in a sliding, high-speed fall, they're much more likely to stay in place than knee pads that strap on with two strips of Velcro.

The sliding gained by the hard plastic exterior helps to deflect some of the impact of a high-speed fall, but only if the knee pad stays firmly fixed over your knee. My own preference is for the more expensive but thicker, sleeved knee pads used by aggressive skaters. The exterior shell is broad and smooth for best sliding. Some fancier lightweight pads designed as "fitness" gear may look less bulky but have less cushion and may not slide as well.

ELBOW PADS

As with knee pads, you should choose elbow pads by imagining your full body weight landing on those bony joints. Because they're higher up, elbows usually hit with more impact than knees. Again, sleeve-style pads stay in place better than strap-ons. Although you can wear them comfortably under loose-fitting sleeves, remember that a fall might tear a hole in the fabric where the pad hits the pavement. Wearing pads over long sleeves makes them a little more slip-prone.

HIP AND TAIL BONE PROTECTION

Some people and some situations (skate camp, for instance) require extra protection for the pelvis bones. As of this writing, available products range from inexpensive hip pads that you insert in your clothes to stretchy shorts with removable tailbone and hip padding. The easiest (but possibly bulky) solution is to go to your local ice- or roller-hockey outfitter and buy a pair of padded pants to wear under baggy shorts.

If you are one who shops on the Internet, search for "padded shorts" or "crash pads."

Accessories and clothes

ATTIRE

Some skate retailers also carry skating clothes and accessories. In general, remember that stretchy or loose-fitting clothes are the most comfortable choice. Jeans are not very comfortable for skating because they bunch up and absorb sweat under a knee pad.

Bike shorts and spandex tights are good for fitness and recreational skating. Baggy T-shirts and even baggier shorts are a favorite uniform among aggressive skaters because,

besides demonstrating an attitude, it allows them to wear heavy-duty padding underneath while practicing tricks. Speed skaters and hockey players have their own specialized outfits, too, usually available in shops where their gear and skates are sold.

Cover up bare arms and legs at first. You can relax this standard as you get more proficient. Save your flashy new skating togs until after you gain better coordination. Avoid wearing black if you think it will make you too hot on sunny days.

> **TIPS FOR SKATING IN THE WORLD**
> When skating in colder temperatures, a pair of dry socks and a sweat shirt in your car can prevent an après-skate chill following a long, sweaty work out.

When skating in low-light conditions, wear a white or light-colored top. Better yet, purchase reflective products such as tape that can be applied to clothes or gear, reflective vests or flashing reflectors.

Dress kids in bright clothes to make them more visible. When you buy your child's helmet, slap a few awesome decals on it to make it more fun to wear.

PACKING YOUR SKATE BAG

Planning an in-line excursion? On cold days, dress in layers you can remove as you warm up. Wear sunscreen no matter what the weather, and take along a pair of sunglasses.

For longer skate trips, bring your pack-mounted hydration system, or, at a minimum, a fanny pack with a bottle of water. It's surprising how dehydrated you can become; your body will be working hard even when you're cooled by the breezes and absorbed in the fun. Make sure you remind the little ones to drink, too.

With so much stuff, you'll want to stay organized. Keep all of your gear in a sport bag. This becomes especially important with every skater you add to your household or car. Besides the items mentioned above, other things to toss in the bag are:

- dry socks and a towel
- skate or ski boot carrier
- windbreaker or sweatshirt
- skate maintenance tools
- a spare heel brake
- this book

CHAPTER 4

Beginning Skills

The skills in this chapter qualify you to skate in flat or gently sloped public places without endangering yourself or others. If you're just learning, don't expect to be comfortable with all of the skills in a day, or even a week. It takes a while to get used to these new demands on your strength, agility, and balance.

Throughout this chapter, key terms are in **bold**. See "Key Terms" on page 17.

Most people can expect a bit of lower leg stiffness for one or two days, until those muscles get accustomed to the new activity. Your feet and shins are likely to be burning within ten minutes of starting due to tension and new muscular uses. That's the time to sit down and re-lace and buckle your skates. Don't skate more than two hours your first time out.

Throughout the remainder of this book, the instructions to skate at a "moderate speed" mean you need to be going fast enough so your internal balance mechanism kicks in, but not so fast that you are afraid to try anything new.

In-line fundamentals

What it is: Stances, terms, falling, getting up.
How to learn: Eight mini-lessons on the carpet.

Read this entire section in one sitting to familiarize yourself with the key terms and fundamental components of in-line skating. Perform the drills at home on a nice cushy carpet, safe from harm and hidden from a grinning audience!

THE READY POSITION
The in-line ready position is the most important fundamental for the beginning skater. It is the same centered, semi-crouch used for tennis and skiing, among many other sports. This athletic, bent-knee position gives your body room to react in unexpected situations.

Without the ready position, any surprise is bound to lead to an unwelcome meeting with the pavement. Once you become conscious of your body and how to keep it "in line," your skating skills will improve with every hour you're on skates.

Reduce balance problems by teaching yourself what the right position feels like—as well as how the wrong position feels, and how to correct it immediately. That awareness will give you the confidence you need to pursue the remaining skills in this book.

Without skates, stand in front of a full-length mirror and watch your body as you assume the ready position:

1. Place feet shoulder-width apart.

2. Raise both hands to waist level within your peripheral vision.

3. Flex (bend) ankles, knees and hips so you sink a few inches.

4. Turn sideways and look in the mirror to be sure your shoulders are over your hips, and your hips are over your ankles.

5. When you look down, your knees should block the view of your toes.

6. Next, close your eyes to test your equilibrium and get a sense of the position from within. Take a deep breath. As you exhale, become as relaxed in the upper body as possible. Try to memorize how this feels, noticing the different muscles involved.

7. Open your eyes and look at the mirror again. Sink lower over your heels by bending your knees and ankles to get into a more aggressive stance. As your behind moves back, notice how your shoulders drop slightly forward to maintain the even forward-to-back weight distribution.

8. Return to your original ready position. Try leaning forward, then backward. When you skate with your weight too far over your toes, your knees straighten—the cause of most beginner falls. Straight knees also lead to backward falls.

9. Tuck your pelvis forward slightly. When you get your first taste of skating, you will likely be tempted to arch your back in fear. Resist! Get used to correcting this now by tucking the bottom half of your pelvis forward.

Well-bent knees are crucial to in-line skating. They provide a platform of stability from which you can respond by moving either up or down, depending on the situation. With knees already straight, the usual upward response of a startled beginning skater leads directly to a backward fall, risking a painfully bruised tail bone.

Bent knees are also necessary to achieve stroke effectiveness. With straight knees, your stroke power and efficiency is limited to the few inches the skate can remain in contact with the pavement. Bent knees deliver longer, more powerful strokes.

But the biggest incentive for you right now is that with bent knees, the heel brake works effectively. With straight knees it just doesn't do the job because you lack proper leverage.

STANDING UP FOR THE FIRST TIME

If it's within your control, do not try getting up from a sitting position on the floor or pavement the very first time you try on skates. A bench or a hard chair with arms will make this adventure much easier, whether you're in a rental shop or in your own home.

On a non-rolling surface, you should have no fear of standing upright, but if you do need to hold onto the back of a chair or place your hand on a wall, go ahead.

1. Put on your protective gear (yes, *really!*) and the skates.

2. Place your skates into a **V stance** (toes out, heels touching), and move to the edge of the seat so your hips are directly over your heels.

3. With hands on the edge of a bench or gripping the arms of the chair, rise straight up in one fluid motion, leaning forward only enough to center your weight directly over your feet.

4. Feel your way into the in-line skating ready position you tried at the mirror.

Do you feel any pressure or discomfort in your boots? It's a lot easier to learn how to skate when you aren't in pain! If there's a problem, try opening, adjusting, and refastening. Make sure your socks have no wrinkles, too. Besides discomfort, wrinkles can also cause blisters when skating.

Once you're comfortable, proceed through the following drills on a plush, non-rolling surface to experience and learn the names of each in-line fundamental.

KEY TERMS AND MOVES

1. Standing with feet close and parallel, bend knees and ankles (with pelvis tucked under you) to sink six inches or so, and then rise up and down once or twice more. There should be a slight resistance of the boot against the front of your shins as you sink, offering a comforting feeling of stability. As you continue with this drill, pay attention to how the **pressure** under your wheels changes as your body position changes. Pressure is fundamental to in-line skating.

2. To test your **balance**, starting from the **ready position**, carefully bend your knees so you can reach them with your hands, and then continue on down to

touch your toes. Observe how mobile you are on in-line skates, and how maintaining balance is possible in different positions (on the carpet, at least). Return to an upright position.

3. Tip both skates onto the right wheel **edges** and then the left. Experience the sturdy lateral ankle support of your skate cuffs (but don't look down if you want to keep your balance!). By tipping both skates in the same direction, you are pressuring **corresponding edges**.

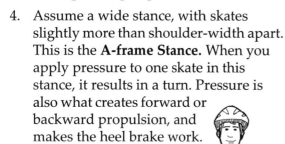

4. Assume a wide stance, with skates slightly more than shoulder-width apart. This is the **A-frame Stance.** When you apply pressure to one skate in this stance, it results in a turn. Pressure is also what creates forward or backward propulsion, and makes the heel brake work.

5. Allow both knees to tip inward. Your skates will be on their **inside edges**. These are the edges you will use to push off against when you first learn how to get rolling.

6. Untip and return to a shoulder-width stance. Rotate your head, torso and

raised hands to the left and then to the right. **Rotation** is a fundamental component of almost every turning skill.

7. Relax your ankles and tip both skates outward, onto the **outside edges**. As your skills improve, you will find uses for your outside edges, such as for Crossover Turns and Parallel Turns.

8. Shift all of your weight to the left skate, bend your knee, and extend your right skate directly to the side as far right as you can reach and still be in contact with the ground. The left leg has become your **support leg**, and the right, simulating the correct angle of an efficient stroke, has performed as the **action** leg. In almost every in-line skill, one leg provides support and balance while the other performs the maneuver that results in a turn, propulsion or other

Beginning Skills

skill. Return to a shoulder-width stance. The illustration below shows a more typical action and support leg stance.

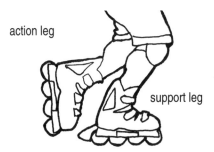

action leg

support leg

9. Arrange your skates with toes together and heels out. This is the **A-Stance**, a narrow version of the A-frame stance; it's used in making backward Swizzles (see page 89).

THE SAFE-T

There are many situations in which you need to be able to anchor your feet and stand still—for instance, when you're chatting with friends, or waiting at an intersection for cars to pass or the light to change. There is a better way to do this than hugging the stoplight pole!

1. Roll the heel of the brakeless boot (for most people, that's the left) in close until it is touching the arch of the other boot.

2. With knees slightly bent, try to shove your heels back to

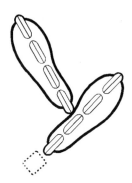

wedge both skates more snugly into the **Safe-T,** which keeps your feet from rolling. It doesn't have to be a perfect letter T. You can use a smaller angle if that makes you feel more secure.

Be sure to assume a Safe-T the first time you stand on a rolling surface.

Once your one-footed balance improves adequately, another option for standing still is to engage the heel brake either by tipping up a the braking toe or scissoring an ABT skate forward. (See "Try the braking foot position" on page 68.)

HOW TO FALL

Indulge in a pain-free fall before you begin learning to skate in earnest. Having confidence in your protective gear will greatly enhance your in-line learning.

1. Stand with skates shoulder-width apart and parallel.

2. Bend down and put your hands near your toes.

3. Fingers raised, reach forward toward the carpet or lawn until you topple over your front wheels.

4. You will automatically land on your knees and then your hands. Bang those knee and elbow pads a couple more times for good measure. Doesn't that cushion feel good? In an emergency situation, you may need to deliberately hit the pavement this way to avoid serious injury. Even a controlled fall demonstrates why thick knee pads and sturdy wrist guards are important safety gear.

5. Since you were undoubtedly over-cautious the first time down, be sure to repeat this safe fall as soon as you learn how to get up, and again the first time you stand on pavement.

When you feel a fall coming while actually skating, do your best to be like a cat. Twist around to get your hands near your knees and land where the most padding is. Sometimes just grabbing your knee pads is enough to prevent a crash landing.

HOW TO GET UP

There are two ways to get back on your feet.

1. Start from "all fours," on your hands and knees.

2. Lift one knee and place the skate of that foot on the ground, close to your other knee.

3. Get your torso upright so you can sit on the heel of the foot with the knee still on the ground. Make your lower body's contact area with the ground as small as possible so your feet won't roll out from under you on rising.

4. Now, leading with your head, rise straight up in one quick and fluid motion. (If you need added oomph, place both hands on the raised knee and push down on it to get a boost.)

If you are not yet strong enough or stable enough on your skates for the first method, here is an easier way to get up:

1. Start from "all fours" as above.

2. Lift one knee and place the skate of that foot on the pavement, with the knee wedged at an outward angle.

3. Remaining upright, place both hands on the ground between your knees.

4. Now, do your best to look like a frog: Using your hands on the ground for support, raise the second knee and pull that skate under you so you end up in a deep squat. Resist croaking.

5. Try to lock your skates into a Safe-T before you raise your hips and head on the way up to standing.

DRY LAND DUCK WALK

To make in-line skates go forward, you must push off from your inside wheel edges.

1. Assume the V-stance (toes out, heels touching).

2. Standing in place, lift one skate at a time, shifting your weight right, left, right, left. Take care to keep that V-Stance.

3. Begin to move forward by advancing each skate a few inches ahead. The weight shift with your feet so close together will require you to waddle like a duck. (This time, resist quacking!)

4. Feel the pressure along the inside of your arch as you push against each skate's inside edges to move forward. Remember to keep those knees bent!

5. Try to set each skate down almost in a Safe-T to head off the habit of an unnecessarily wide stance.

CRAB STEPS

Here's a great way to learn about pressure on your outside edges.

1. Stand in your best ready position on an imaginary (or real) line that passes from left to right under your skates.

2. Turn and look up the line to your left. With arms raised and wide, rotate your shoulders and hands toward the left, too.

3. Pick up the right skate and pass it across the left to place it back on the lawn or carpet on the line.

4. As your body crosses over it, totally relax your left ankle and allow the left skate to flop way over onto its outside edge.

5. To untangle yourself, retrieve the tipped left skate and place it upright on the line just beyond the right skate's position.

6. Lean the way with your left hip as you step up the line. To make the crossover easier, try to rotate your pelvis toward the line, too, so your right leg has less distance to cross.

7. Repeat, working your way up the line. Remember, although the upper body is twisted toward the direction of travel, your skates remain pointed across (perpendicular to) the line.

8. Without turning around, return to your starting point by traveling back down your line in the opposite direction.

CARPET SKATING

We've done everything else on the carpet, why not skate, too? It's a great way to get a feel for the proper foot positioning and the push that makes a glide, but in a very safe environment. You can do this on grass, too, as long as it's dry.

1. Assume the Safe-T position.

2. Tip the back skate (the top part of the T) onto its inside edge behind you. Concentrate on pushing against that edge, as you…

3. Lean your upper body over the knee of the front skate and lunge forward in the style of a fencing enthusiast.

4. When most of your weight has been transferred to the lunging skate, pick up the back skate and close the gap between your feet.

• This is known as **recovery**, and it's very important to close the gap as much as possible before you return the recovered skate to the ground to start a new stride. Otherwise, you'll end up lurching around with short, stiff-legged strokes looking like some modern day Frankenstein. "Frankenskating" is the hallmark of beginners who got their start on in-lines without proper instruction.

5. Place the recovered skate back down slightly ahead of the previous front skate. Repeat the push, lean and lunge, with it in front, angling your upper body toward the new direction.

6. Recover and repeat, starting each stroke by pushing against the inside edge of the back skate's wheels. Try to match the Stride One diagram on the facing page.

Stride One (the beginning stride)

What it is: Beginning forward motion and standard technique for slat bridges, slick or rough pavement.
How to learn: Two rolling drills.

It's time to put the urethane to the road. Don your skates and safety gear while seated on a bench or chair next to the pavement, or while seated on the lawn. Get up and, if you're not on the pavement, step onto it and immediately assume the Safe-T.

Before you do anything else, repeat the drills from the preceding pages, especially falling down and getting up!

DUCK WALK

The purpose of this drill is not to make you look like a duck (and yes, it will!), but to teach you how to transfer your weight from one skate to the other in good skating form.

1. Starting from the Safe-T, do your best to repeat the duck walk exactly as you did on the carpet. Step right, left, right and left, in very short steps.

2. Advance each skate a few inches each time you return it to the pavement.

3. Feel your weight in your right, then left heel. Concentrate on keeping your toes pointed out as you set each heel back down under your belly button.

4. If you begin to roll, relax into a coasting ready position and try to enjoy these first fruits of your labor.

STRIDE ONE

Stride One lets you feel the stroking fundamentals that apply at every level of skating: weight on the heels, pushing to the side instead of back, and setting the skate down directly below your body weight.

Skaters of *all* abilities resort to this short, quick stride on wet, slippery pavement or very rough surfaces. That's because it's easier to keep moving forward without slipping or stalling as long as you keep your skates close under your body. In this Stride One diagram, the filled in areas indicate wheel pressure.

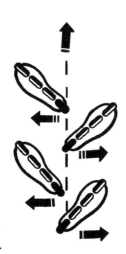

1. Building on the duck walk, start pushing against the back skate's inside edge as preparation for transferring the weight to the front skate. That pressure results in a short **glide**. The combination of pressure and glide becomes a **stride**. If you have any ice or roller skating history at all, now is the moment the familiar feeling will kick in.

2. Keep your strides short enough so that you can maintain your balance. If you build too much speed, relax into a coasting ready position until you're ready to resume striding. Your lesson location is flat as a pancake, right?

3. Do your best to keep your knees bent and maintain an upright (not bent forward) ready position.

4. Got a weak side? To concentrate on the weaker push, use a **scooter**-style stroke: Using your strongest stroking foot as your support leg, use the weaker foot to repeatedly push off and recover. Practice

this every time you skate to equalize your stride.

Practice Tip
Spend the rest of this day's session getting used to Stride One. Call it a day if your ankles become too tired to keep your skates upright on the pavement.

Hey, is this fun or what?!

If the sport of in-line skating or this much balance work is all new to you, you may find yourself getting beyond your comfort zone, and as a result, beginning to bend forward at the waist. This happens when your lower back becomes taut with tension. Any lower back stiffness you feel after your first day of skating will be due to this common beginner's reaction. Take heart in the fact that the confidence that comes from practice and skating in a good ready position will cure this in no time. Meanwhile, keep your sessions short and be sure to stretch afterward.

Of course, the *real* liberation will come the day you learn how to control your speed and stop using that little rubber brake pad! Be patient, that time is coming soon.

EMERGENCY STOPS

You have no business skating near traffic or on trails before you learn how to stop and control your speed. That said, the following four emergency techniques will work for the novice skater moving at slow speeds in a protected environment, such as an empty parking lot.

- At very slow speeds on level ground, simply relax and roll. Steer your toes together; when they meet they will stop rolling. This is not an option on hills or when obstacles are ahead.

- Only if moving very slowly, roll up to something stationary you can grab. (But watch out: If you're going too fast, your feet will keep on going without you!)

- If in imminent danger, pitch forward and slide on padded hands and knees.

- If skating next to a lawn (or even dirt or bark), step off the pavement and take one or two quick running steps.

After you learn the heel brake, use the above methods at your own discretion.

Heel brake stop

What it is: Stopping and preventing unwanted speed with a standard or ABT brake.
How to learn: Three non-rolling stances followed by five rolling drills for the approach, touchdown, finishing move and speed control.

Most people are discouraged to find they don't get the feel for stopping with a heel brake right away. Yet, when used with the proper form, it can be the most immediate and powerful stopping tool you'll ever need. Unfortunately, some skaters never figure out how to use it, and many of these folks actually remove it altogether. This is not going to happen to you!

Someday you may be tempted to remove your heel brake, too. This is not wise for recreational, skate-to-ski or fitness skaters, who deal with hills, intersections, and traffic, and often must share favorite paths with an unpredictable crowd. Hockey and aggressive skaters manage successfully without a heel brake because they have learned to use Lunge Stops, T-Stops and Power Slides to

slow down and stop effectively. Speed skaters sacrifice the extra weight of a brake for the sake of speed, and rely on T-Stops, agility and sheer luck for downhills.

ABOUT THE HEEL BRAKE DRILLS

In *Before You Roll*, you will start getting used to the all-important braking stance while standing still. Next, the drills in *Stopping on Pavement* will let you piece together the approach, the brake touch-down and the finishing move.

For the best results, focus on these three points:

- Approach your stops **low** and **narrow** (ready position with knees touching), and then get **long** (the Scissors Stance). This stance keeps the weight of your body behind that little rubber stopper, compounding the friction.
  Low, narrow and *long*: Words to stop by!

- If your skates have a cuff-activated (ABT) brake, consult your user manual to adjust the pad very close to the ground so you'll have "instant gratification" when learning to stop. You can raise it again later if it gets in the way. As your skill and confidence grow, try lifting your toe to stop the standard way.

- Constantly scan the pavement ahead when the heel brake is engaged so you can release it for raised sidewalk slabs or any debris that might catch the brake and send you flying. Raise the brake temporarily to roll across slippery debris such as gravel and wet leaves.

BEFORE YOU ROLL

Try the braking posture

The most effective heel brake stops begin from a solid ready position. To find the braking posture, start by reviewing your ready position on a lawn or carpet. Your upper body is upright and your hips, knees and ankles are bent. Do not lean forward or arch your back. Instead, curve your spine slightly so that your pelvis is tucked in. This brings your hips forward under your body, making it easier to extend the braking foot.

Try the Scissors Stance

Besides serving as an approach for heel brake stops, the scissors stance is the best position for gliding safely and easily over nasty patches of pavement. In this stance your wheels form a longer platform that gives you more front-to-back stability, which means you have more room to lurch when rolling over a crack or rough patch. Best of all, you are already very close to the stopping position, should you need it.

1. Assume the ready position, with knees well bent, feet shoulder-width apart.

2. Shift your weight over to the supporting leg, keeping the braking skate in place.

3. Moving *only* your brake leg from the knee down, push that skate forward keeping the toe down. It won't go very far if your supporting knee is too straight. From the side view, your lower legs should form a triangle (see photo). Make sure your skates are parallel and no more than 4 inches apart so your toes are both pointing forward. This is the Scissors Stance: *low, narrow* and *long*.

Try the braking foot position

Depending on your brake type, *one* of the following moves will engage the brake. Don't look at your feet as you try the appropriate foot position for your brake. Leaning forward takes you out of the braking posture, which results in less balance and braking friction regardless of brake type.

Standard heel brake: Starting in the Scissors Stance, lift the toe until the brake touches down. Be sure to bend your supporting knee enough so that the brake skate can be pushed well ahead of your body mass.

Cuff-activated brake: The simple act of sliding your braking skate into the Scissors Stance described above in step 3 causes the brake to touch the ground. Instead of lifting your toe, you must consciously press your big toe *down* toward the pavement, the same way a diver or ballerina points the toes. Doing this helps you use your calf muscle to move the cuff backward as your foot slides

forward. Pressure on the back of your calf lets you know you are pushing the brake down so the rubber can drag on the pavement.

For either type of brake, at some point in the future, you may need to transfer *all* of your weight onto the heel brake and lift the trailing skate off the ground. At higher speeds, this is the weight transfer that results in an expeditious stop. Try this on the lawn now.

STOPPING ON PAVEMENT

Now that you have let your body experience the braking positions standing still, it's time to piece them together in braking sequence.

The approach

There are two parts to the approach: relaxing into a coasting ready position, and then sliding into the Scissors Stance.

1. Stroke to gain a moderate speed.

2. Stop stroking and relax into a coasting ready position. See how far you can roll in good form (the slower you go, the worse your balance).

3. Repeat until you can coast a few feet, then begin pulling your knees inward so they can touch. This is important feedback for that necessary narrow stance. Once you can coast 10 feet with knee pads touching...

4. Shift your weight to your support leg and slide into your Scissors Stance by pushing your braking skate ahead with all wheels still touching the pavement. Cuff-activated brakers, if you feel a drag, pull the skate back toward you slightly (it's eager to do its job!).

5. Hold steady and continue to coast in the Scissors Stance. If you lose your balance, bring the brake skate back under your hips until you're stable, and then scissors it forward again. Remember, keeping hands in view at waist level gives you better balance.

Practice Tips

• Try squeezing your knee pads together. This forms a more solid foundation for better stability and balance, and is very helpful if you keep veering off to one side or the other.

- Spend as much time as you need on this drill to get used to the Scissors Stance, which will be a key defensive posture from now on. It may be difficult to keep your skates close together at first. This takes a bit of balance but definitely becomes easier with practice.

- Still shaky? Try working on the Marching and Training Wheel drills listed under "One-footed balance" on page 82.

- The slower you roll, the harder it is to stay balanced. Dare to coast a bit faster.

- Bounce up and down over your support skate to get a feel for the technique and hip muscles you will be using for the finishing move of braking.

Heel brake touch downs
Let's put the rubber to the road. We'll start with very light brake dragging to improve your balance in the braking position.

1. Skate forward to get the speed necessary to coast for 10 to 15 feet.

2. Make your best braking approach in a low, narrow and long Scissors Stance.

3. Your brake type determines how you accomplish the touch-downs:

   - **Standard brake (photo).** Lift the toe of the brake skate until the rubber touches down. Let it drag audibly but only very lightly on the pavement. If necessary, drop your toe to regain balance, then lift and drag again. Tip the toe up and down as you coast. Your goal is to roll several feet while dragging the brake lightly.

   - **Cuff-activated brakes.** Press the big toe in the braking skate down onto the pavement as you scissors that boot ahead, making sure to "hunker down" over the support foot rather than leaning forward over the brake. As the toe is pointed and pushed forward, the back of the calf presses the boot cuff, which presses the brake to pavement. Feel the vibrations of your brake lightly dragging, and then bring the skate back under you.

4. Starting from lots of touch downs, try keeping the brake down for increasing distances of light dragging.

5. For now, try to hear and prolong the
   light contact rather than trying to stop.

Note for cuff-activated brakers
If your brake pad doesn't touch the ground
when you scissors, try lowering it closer to
the ground (see your owner's manual). If
that doesn't help, increase the angle of your
braking leg. The calf cannot be perpendicular to the pavement. If it is, you are lunging
forward with your upper body instead of
pushing the brake forward.

Finishing the stop
Save this drill for when you can drag your
brake lightly for at least five feet.

1. Once again, approach in your best Scissors Stance with weight mostly on the
   back skate. Start a light brake drag.

2. Begin straightening the brake skate's
   knee and pushing the brake pad forward
   (not down). Try to keep that skate as
   close as possible to the middle of your
   line of travel (known as the **centerline**).

3. To assertively finish the stop, drop your
   hips as though trying to sit down on the
   heel of your back support skate. As long
   as you don't lean forward, this "down
   bounce" bends your support knee so
   much that it "squirts" the brake forward
   at the same time, adding friction.

4. Quickly straighten up as soon as you
   stop so you won't fall over.

Practice Tips
You have just mastered the approach, touch
down and finish of a heel brake stop. Now
all you need is practice!

- **To fight a skipping brake,** get the brake
  pad well ahead of your shoulders, and
  make sure you increase the pressure
  very gradually. This is the hardest trick
  to learn once you've mastered the other
  braking skills. Squeeze the brake on the
  same way you do the brake pedal in a
  car as you approach a stop sign.

- **To fight the upper body's forward
  motion,** tighten your stomach muscles in
  anticipation as you begin to add pressure. Concentrate on sinking down
  behind the brake as the pressure
  increases, as though you are about to sit
  on a stool, keeping shoulders above the
  hips. Keep your head up and eyes forward. The moment your shoulders and
  head fall ahead of the brake, lost leverage makes it almost impossible to get
  enough pressure for an effective stop.

- **To fight the tendency to swerve off
  course**, make sure your skates remain
  perfectly parallel with each other and no
  more than hip width apart. This ensures
  that as you slow to a stop, it will be in a
  straight line. If you angle the braking
  foot off to the side, you'll swerve that
  way. Try squeezing your knees together.
  As your balance improves, this will no
  longer be a problem.

STOP ON A LINE (100 TIMES)

You will never be able to stop on a dime with today's in-line heel brake technology. However, *you can stop wherever you want* as long as you stay alert enough to plan ahead.

This drill lets you know how far ahead you must begin braking maneuvers to be able to stop exactly where you want. If you repeat it at least 100 times—making test stops anywhere and everywhere—you will learn to use the brake instinctively. That is what leads to the confidence and balance that lets you skate in a world filled with intersections, pedestrians, cyclists and cars.

1. Spot a line in a parking lot or game court and start skating toward it.

2. Make your best Scissors Stance approach and engage the brake with light pressure. When the line is no more than two feet away, drop your hips and "smear" the heel brake forward. Don't worry if you don't quite stop or veer off to the side on the first try.

3. Try again, adjusting how far in advance of the line you need to start the coast, engage the brake and drop the hips.

4. Work to shorten your stopping distances by increasing the brake pressure and making the hip drop sooner and harder.

Practice Tips

- With each successful stop right on the line, go back and try another from a faster approach. Work to become more and more assertive as you practice stopping in your safe location.

- As a good confidence builder, find a very short, gently sloped driveway (out of traffic flow) and practice making complete stops before entering the street.

- If you can't help leaning forward, put both hands on your braking knee and push down to make up for the leverage and friction you lose in that posture.

- Don't be tentative: "Squash the triangle" below your knees to really finish the stop where you want.

- Don't quit trying if you don't feel confident in your stopping abilities the first day or week; good technique comes when you have good balance, and that comes with a few hours on skates.

In-line heel brakes really do work, and they are just as important for safety as your wrist guards or helmet. Practice braking until you feel the freedom and assurance that comes with knowing you are in complete control.

CRUISE CONTROL

In addition to serving as a stopping tool, your heel brake helps you avoid unintended acceleration. If you don't learn this braking variation, you may find yourself taking a dive to the pavement in a panic. For slalom skaters, this technique manages the speed without disrupting the rhythm of linked downhill turns. Of course, you should be able to fully stop on flat ground before approaching any slope.

Learn this skill on a long, gentle slope with a gradual leveling-off at the bottom. If you do get going too fast to want to use your brake, make an A-frame Turn or use one of the emergency stops described on page 66.

1. Start coasting down the slope.

2. Immediately scissors into the heel brake position *before* you pick up speed.

3. Drag the brake lightly all the way down, maintaining a straight path.

4. Balancing mostly on the support leg, adjust the heel brake pressure so that you are rolling fast enough for good balance but not so fast you get scared.

Practice until you can engage and release the brake whenever you want, whether to stop or to maintain a safe speed downhill. Be sure to release the brake to roll safely over raised cracks or anything that might grab it.

A-frame Turn

What it is: Beginning turn in a wide stance.
How to learn: One stationary drill, one rolling.

Much of the elegance of in-line skating comes from gliding through smooth turns with both skates on the ground.

BEFORE YOU ROLL
Practice these turning motions on the lawn.

1. Stand in the A-frame Stance, with skates at least 18" apart (see page 60).

2. Hands raised to waist high, rotate your head, shoulders, hands and hips toward the left. Always enter a turn head-first by looking in the new direction of travel.

3. Push against the right skate's inside edge. When you're rolling, this pressure will cause a turn to the left.

4. Now slide the right skate about one foot ahead, steering it in an arc toward the

---

TIPS FOR SKATING IN THE WORLD
Use your head. Looking in your new direction makes turns tighter and easier.

left. This simulates how your lower body joins your upper body's rotation during an actual rolling turn. Return the skate to its original wide-stance position.

5. Repeat this several times on both sides to feel how to steer both the right and left skate into a turn.

THE TURN

Turning is a result of pressure against the sides of the wheels when the skate is tipped, known as edging. If you have ever skied, you will recognize the A-frame as the "snowplow" or "wedge" turn.

1. In an open area, build up enough speed to coast 10 feet.

2. Starting from a coasting ready position, push your skates into the A-frame Stance, with feet wider than shoulders.

3. Without leaning over, rotate your head, shoulders, hands and hips toward the left, and press against the inside edge of your right skate at the same time. Good upper body rotation and a wide A-frame stance results in a successful left turn.

4. Practice making different sized turns, starting big and working toward smaller turns by making your A-frame narrower and adding more pressure to the right foot.

5. Now work on your turns to the right. In both directions, try to spin like a top: upright keeps it spinning but a tilt (leaning into the turn) stops the spin.

With just a little practice, A-Frame turns seem to happen almost naturally.

Stride Two (the basic stride)

What it is: Basic forward motion for cruising
How to learn: One rolling drill

Now that you know how to use the heel brake to stop, it's safe to improve the efficiency of your stroke so you can roll faster. This happens when you add more pressure to the inside edge at push-off, and keep the pushing skate in contact with the pavement for a greater distance and longer amount of time. Warm up with Stride One.

1. Skating forward, get "shorter" by bending your knees to bring your hips closer to your heels.

- *Bent knees* allow your stroking skate to be in contact with the pavement farther, a main source of power.

2. Prolong each glide by counting "one-two-three" before starting a new stroke.

   - *Longer glides* give you more time to complete farther strokes.

3. If you dare, try to push harder to stroke.

   - Increased *stroke pressure* creates more power and speed.

4. Try to keep the heel wheel on the pavement as long as possible for each stroke, and push to the side instead of back.

5. Retrieve the stroking heel fully beneath your belly button each time you set the skate back down to begin another stroke.

Practice Tips

- **If you feel unstable**, raise your hands to waist level and within view.

- **If you have a stiff, lurching stride**, bend your knees more, get upright instead of leaning forward, and try to fully recover the stroking skate (feel your knee pads brush together before set down). And bend your knees even more!

- **If you can't balance on one foot** long enough to count to three, practice gliding from half strokes: Support yourself on one leg and stroke repeatedly with the other leg as though you were riding a scooter. Practice on both sides but do more on the weaker side.

Swizzle

What it is: Forward propulsion by using both feet to trace hourglass shapes on the pavement.
How to learn: Two rolling drills.

You are about to find out why fitness skaters love the Swizzle: be prepared for some soreness in the inner thigh and possibly other muscles. (This is a good thing!)

EXPERIENCE SWIZZLE PROPULSION

1. In a V-Stance, put your knee pads together and push them two inches forward, letting the skates tilt. Your body sinks a few inches in response.

2. With eyes and hands up, push sideways against both sets of tipped inside edges. As your legs unbend and heels separate, forward propulsion results.

3. To avoid doing the splits as you try this, do your best to keep your knees close together, and simply roll until you stop.

Practice Tip

Imagine you are standing in the center of a large clock with 12 o'clock straight ahead of you. When you swizzle, you want to push your right skate's heel wheel towards 3 o'clock while simultaneously pushing your left skate's heel wheel towards 9 o'clock.

LINKED SWIZZLES

Linked swizzles alternate between the A-Stance and V-Stance.

1. Repeat steps 1 and 2 above to start moving, keeping your weight on the heels.

2. Before your legs straighten wide, begin to steer into a pigeon-toed A-Stance. This is possible when your toes are light and your heels are heavy.

3. Use your inner thigh muscles if necessary to pull the skates back to hip width.

4. When your skates are close and parallel, "coil" your legs into pushing position by bending your knees.

5. Tip both skates onto their inside edges and immediately start another heel press toward 9 and 3 o'clock.

6. Steer both toes back to center before your legs fully straighten. Seek the momentum that is the reward of rhythm.

Practice Tips

If you can't pull your legs back together:

- You have too much weight on the front wheels; push off with heel wheels only.

- You are pushing your knees too far out: try to push only with your heels so that your knees can stay close together.

- Your push is tentative. Be brave!

- You are not bending and straightening your knees rhythmically. Rhythmic motion is the key to swizzling success, because that is what allows you to take maximum advantage of the energy generated by uncoiling your legs. Chant "one-two-three, one-two-three" as you link swizzles to make repeated hourglass figures on the pavement.

Spin stop

What it is: Using a spin to end forward motion.
How to learn: One rolling drill and practice.

The spin stop evolves out of the basic A-frame Turn, so master that first. The key here is learning to *pivot* on the trailing skate's toe wheel as you shift into a heel-to-heel position.

1. From a moderate speed, begin a left A-frame Turn, rotating your head and shoulders counterclockwise.

2. As the turn weights your right skate, raise the left heel (only) and balance on that toe wheel as you shift the heel in.

3. Once you are heel-to-heel, both toes pointed outward, set the heel down.

4. Settle onto both skates and center your weight evenly between both thighs.

5. You will spin counterclockwise and stop within one rotation.

Practice Tips

Don't expect success on the first try: a lot is going on here! Most problems stem from leaning toward the turn and keeping the knees too close together. Here are some tips to help your "spin cycle:"

- Briefly drag the left toe wheel behind you as you enter the left turn. That friction will pull your knees apart.

- Think of the left foot as trailing *behind* you, not *beside* you.

- Your starting A-frame needs a very wide stance while you're learning how to shift your weight for spinning success.

- The left toe wheel stays in contact with the pavement throughout the move!

- Don't lean or tip shoulders to the left or that skate will be too heavy to pivot on.

- If you are still picking up the left skate, practice this toe-pivot "dance move" while standing still. Start in a wide A-frame Stance, arms outstretched. Tip the left skate's heel up and, pressing on the toe, rotate the heel in and set it back down. Tip and rotate it back out to the original position. Shift it back and forth, in and out, using weight on the toe to keep your balance. *Shake that booty!*

Grass stop

What it is: Using lawn to end forward movement.
How to learn: One rolling drill.

If your practice area is bordered by lawn, you are lucky. Knowing how to make a grass stop allows you to be more daring. Make sure the grass is dry, however, because rusty bearings are expensive to replace.

Scout your location: Choose a stretch of sidewalk or any paved area with lawn on at least one side, and at least 10 to 15 feet of paved approach, either straight or at an angle.

1. Approach the lawn, hands at waist level.

2. Scissors one skate forward for more stability, with slightly more weight on the

back leg. (ABT brakers need to scissors the non-brake skate ahead.)

3. The friction of the grass will cause a sudden slow-down. To compensate, tighten your abdominal muscles and shift your weight back as you roll onto the lawn.

4. If necessary, take a few running steps to stay upright on the first try, or fall forward onto your knee pads.

5. Practice until you can roll to a stop on the grass without any rescue actions.

Parallel Turn

What it is: A banked turn on corresponding edges.
How to learn: One stationary, five rolling drills.

The graceful in-line Parallel Turn begins by coasting in a narrow Scissors Stance (think "bicycle configuration"). With enough speed and confidence, simply looking over your shoulder in the proper stance causes your skates to tip onto **corresponding edges** in an effortless banked turn. You can tip quite far without crashing thanks to centrifugal force.

The scary part about learning this turn is that your center of gravity ends up way left of your feet when making a hard left turn! That's why Parallel Turns do not come easily until after several hours of skating.

If the Parallel Turn seems too scary, put off attempting to learn it until you have put in several hours of quality rolling time. You'll be amazed at the difference that will make.

3. Now, rotate your head, shoulders, hands and hips toward the left without releasing your lower body position or leaning forward at the waist. Allow both knees to tip to the left as well. This puts your skate wheels on corresponding (in this case, left) edges. You will hold this position through your first Parallel Turns.

4. Untwist and repeat several times to get a feel for the parallel turn position.

BUILDING DRILLS

Cones warm-up
Warm up by skating through a long row of cones or other markers about six to eight feet apart on level pavement. Start out making wide A-frame Turns. With each lap through the cones, try to progressively narrow your stance. With a bit of practice, you will find yourself completing these easy turns on corresponding edges.

If this cones drill excites you, (you budding "Conehead"!), see the slalom skating instructions on page 94.

1. Coast in a swapped Scissors Stance
This will feel very awkward at first: In a moderate-speed coast, assume the swapped Scissors Stance and align your body over your right side, skates no more than 3 inches apart. Make many practice laps focusing on keeping 3/4 of your weight on the right, rear foot. Bounce up and down over the right leg a few times to really settle your weight on that hip. Except for the bent right knee, you are in a fairly upright stance.

BEFORE YOU ROLL
Prepare yourself first by experiencing the motions of a Parallel Turn while stationary (on pavement, grass or lawn). The following drills favor those who prefer to turn counterclockwise. If that's not you, translate the instructions to learn clockwise first.

1. Starting in a ready position, scissors the left skate forward until the ankle is even with the toes of the other skate. This is a Scissors Stance but with swapped feet.

2. Tuck the right knee pad behind your left knee so that the inside top of your right thigh is slightly covered by the left thigh.

TIPS FOR SKATING IN THE WORLD
Carry some speed to traverse a short
patch of rough pavement or a wood slat
bridge with ease. At a slower pace, the
vibrations and your balance are worse.

Work to align the left heel wheel about an
inch ahead and to the left of the right toe
wheel. This feels like you are about to try to
brake with the wrong foot in front.

2. Lift the front toe
Once you are successfully coasting in the
narrow stance with an upright torso, lift the
left toe and get used to coasting that way.
Again, squeeze those knees and thighs
together and bounce over the back right
skate, feeling your hip muscles working.

3. Add a toe-lifted turn
At a moderate speed in that toe-up coast,
begin looking over your left shoulder as you
try tipping the right knee under your belly
button. Eventually, this should result in a
turn as long as you are maintaining that all-
important narrow Scissors Stance with
wheels in a line, not side by side. Remember
to keep an upright torso—don't lean left or
bend over the left foot. That puts too much
weight on it and kills the turn.

4. Drop the front toe
Once you master the previous three drills,
you are ready to begin dropping the front
toe mid-turn. This is where repeated
attempts really pay off. Keep at it until you
can hold onto your narrow stance (try tucking the back right knee in tight behind the

front left knee). Begin dropping the toe
sooner and sooner in the turn until you can
complete a full parallel turn with all eight
wheels on the pavement. Don't forget to
turn your head to the left, too!

Practice Tips
- Approach the turn with sufficient speed
  to maintain balance. A slightly sloped
  learning area helps with this.

- Go back and spend more time on the
  previous step if you're having trouble.

- Relax and allow your stance, the skates,
  and centrifugal force to do the work for
  you. The harder you work, the harder it
  is to learn this skill.

Your goal is to make a tight 90- to 180-
degree swerve. When you begin to hear the
swooshing sound of your wheels scrubbing
the pavement, you know you've got it!

Parallel Turns require confidence born of
practice. Whether it takes an hour or a
month, this elegant turn is worth the effort.

Mobility and balance drills
What it is: Fast track to better balance and agility.
How to learn: Three one-legged balance drills, get-
ting up and down curbs, rolling crouch and kneel.

Remember these tips as you practice this
chapter's skills and drills for a few weeks:

- Do your best to stay relaxed and in the
  skater's ready position.

- Relieve tension by taking a deep breath
  and then exhaling fully.

- Maintain enough speed to engage your internal "gyroscope." Just as a cyclist can stay balanced as long as those wheels are turning, you need bit of rolling momentum for your skating balance to kick in.

- Work harder on your weak side for every skill so that you will become a balanced skater in every sense of the word.

- If your arches or shins begin to hurt, sit down for a few minutes of rest; loosen your skate buckles or laces to allow the blood to flow more easily.

THE PICK-UP

For safety reasons, it's important that you learn to feel at ease and stay balanced while shifting your center of gravity.

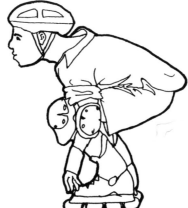

1. In a coasting ready position, reach down to touch your knees, then your toes, and then stand upright. Repeat several times.

2. As your flexibility permits, practice stooping down to pick up leaves, rocks, or twigs off the pavement as you roll by.

3. Switch hands so the muscles on both sides of your body are stimulated.

THE FIRST CURB

Deal with your first curb from a complete stop, both getting up and down.

1. **To get up:** Assume a V-Stance facing the curb and roll one skate against the side at a 45 degree angle, toe wheel touching.

2. Using the curb to prevent the supporting leg from rolling, reach with both hands far forward over the curb. With most of your upper body weight over the curb, lift and place your action skate on the higher surface also angled out at 45 degrees (similar to a Safe-T).

3. A last push from the back support leg pops your weight up and over the curb. Pull that skate up, set it down ahead of the other one, and push off into a glide.

4. **To get down:** Come to a complete stop at the edge, facing sideways to the curb. The skate closest to the curb will be your action skate.

5. Reach down with the action skate as close to the curb as possible, and roll the heel of that skate back against the edge of the curb for stability. A 45-degree angle leaves space for your second skate.

6. Turn slightly to shift all of your weight onto the lower skate and then bring the second down.

7. Reorient both skates forward and stride away. (See "Taking curbs at a roll" on page 109.)

ONE-FOOTED BALANCE

Good one-footed balance enhances your ability to learn more advanced skills and stunts. This does not come easily to beginning skaters, but it is very important from day one, because some degree of supporting leg balance is necessary to use the standard heel brake effectively. Good one-footed balance also means you can step over small obstacles or onto a curb with ease.

Although your balance will automatically improve with time, you can hurry it along in between skating sessions. For example, you can do simple household tasks such as reading your mail, brushing your teeth or watching TV commercials while standing on one foot (not in skates). To challenge yourself even more do these on a wobble or rocker board. Certain Yoga poses also build balance. (See "Balance Poses" on page 137.)

Of course, the best improvements in your skating balance will come from practicing one-footed skating drills. The following three are excellent choices.

Training Wheel

1. Stride to gain a moderate pace, then relax into a coasting ready position.

2. Shift your weight fully over the left foot by aligning your nose and belly button over the left knee and toes.

3. Push your right toe wheel back a few inches and point your toe. This lifts your right heel.

4. Keep one third of your weight on your right toe wheel and let it roll 3 to 6 inches behind your left skate's back wheel.

5. Eliminate wobbles by sitting back slightly to add weight to the right toe.

6. Keep your knee pads close enough to touch each other and the left knee bent for stability.

7. Swap legs and practice the Training Wheel on your other side.

Once you lose your speed, you will find yourself struggling more. When this happens, skate a few strokes to regain your speed for more Training Wheel practice.

Marching

1. Stride to gain a moderate pace.

2. From a coasting ready position, start taking short marching steps, raising each skate only slightly off the ground.

3. Each time you lift a skate, attempt to glide as long as possible on the other. Return to a two-footed coast as needed.

4. As your balance improves, try moving the airborne skate around or extending it ahead, to the side or behind you. Be sure to work on both legs.

5. For extra credit, simulate stepping over obstacles by stepping across a drawn or painted line or over a piece of cord you can feel when you miss and roll over it. Imagine it's a curb or a hose.

Single-Foot Glides

Ballerinas call this an *arabesque*, and artistic skaters call it an *attitude*.

1. Stride to gain a moderate pace and then begin coasting in a ready position.

> **TIPS FOR SKATING IN THE WORLD**
> If you want to skate with your dog on a leash, learn how to use your heel brake. A Spin Stop combined with a leash can have dire consequences!

2. Shift your weight fully over one foot by aligning your nose and belly button directly over it. Slightly flex this knee.

3. Lift the other leg straight out behind you, and then try to straighten both legs.

4. Lift both arms out to the sides and fly like a professional figure skater. Outstretched arms also help you stay balanced on the supporting leg.

5. Glide in this position as long as possible.

6. Be sure to alternate feet. The more attempts you make, the more you improve your balance, regardless of your glide durations.

A CHEAP TRICK: THE KNEEL

If you've had success with the Training Wheel, here's an easy stunt that also builds confidence, balance and mobility. Don't even think about trying this without your knee pads!

1. Stride to gain a moderate pace, then relax into a coasting ready position.

2. Start out with a left-footed Training Wheel where your right heel is the one that's raised.

3. When the right, rear skate is tracking on its front wheel without wobbles, slowly sink straight down into a Kneel, lowering the hips directly over the right upraised heel wheel.

4. As you roll along in the Kneel, balance your weight equally on the right toe wheel and all four of the left skate's wheels.

5. To get up, press the pavement with your right front wheel as you rise straight up. If necessary, push down with both hands on your left knee.

Practice Tips
- For best balance, keep your knees and skates as close together as possible.

- You should be sitting on the back side of the right skate, and both knees should be directly below your chin.

Beginning Skills

CHAPTER 5

Intermediate Skills

To begin working on the lessons in this chapter, you should be comfortable with Stride Two and be able to glide a good distance on one foot. You should be handling curbs, sudden obstacles and rough surfaces without crashing. By now, you should also be able to stop at will on flat pavement within a distance of 15 feet from a cruising speed of up to 8 miles per hour.

In this chapter, you will learn the intermediate maneuvers that require good balance and speed control and make use of your skates' outside edges.

Forward Crossovers

What it is: A speed turn on corresponding edges.
How to learn: One stationary, three rolling drills.

Forward Crossovers let you gracefully round a corner without losing speed. Expect a significant balance challenge, because you must learn to tip your body momentarily outside the stable space between both feet. This is scary enough on your good leg, but it's even trickier on your weak one.

BEFORE YOU ROLL

1. Starting from a ready position, scissors the left skate forward until the ankle is even with the big toe of the other skate.

2. Rotate your torso toward the left and let both knees tip left onto their left edges.

3. Untwist and untilt, and then repeat several times to feel the turning mechanics.

4. Repeat this drill with the right skate forward before learning a right Crossover.

CRAB STEPS ON THE PAVEMENT
Let's repeat the Crab Steps drill (page 63) on pavement. Remember to relax the leading ankle so that the skate tips onto its outside edge as the trailing skate crosses over it.

ASSISTED FIRST CROSSOVERS

Be prepared for success with this drill, because that means you will find yourself accelerating—possibly more than you want!

1. Find a spot on your practice pavement where there is the tiniest slope; parking lot drainage will do just fine.

2. Assume your best bent-knee, totally in-line ready position, standing with your left side toward the decline, and wheels perpendicular to the "fall line," the direction where gravity has its strongest pull.

3. Without changing the position of your feet, rotate your head and waist-high arms so that they are facing the bottom of the decline.

4. Begin making Crab Steps to the left, stepping sideways down the slope.

5. After two Crab Steps, begin to angle your skates slightly down instead of across the slope as you return each skate to the pavement. You will begin to roll with each step.

6. For now, just try to set the right skate down in front of the left skate's toe wheel. You can work on crossing further over later, once your confidence grows.

7. Maintain the upper body's rotation as you resist the impulse to quit stepping or straighten your knees; instead, do your best to maintain your stepping rhythm and twisted upper body.

8. See if you can Crab Step/roll your way around a big circle (to your left) until

you return to your starting place. Remember to keep your chin over your left shoulder, facing the direction of the turn (left). And don't even think about looking at your feet!

Repeat until you can make at least three sequential Crab Steps with wheels rolling. Seek constant pressure along the bottom outside of your left foot (and wheel edges) and along the bottom inside of the right.

CROSSOVERS

Crossover Turns are easier to learn if your practice spot has a large painted circle, such as those found on school playgrounds. It should be15-20 feet in diameter with a center marker for spotting. If you do not have a compliant cat like my Bugaboo, place a cone or other object on the pavement that can serve as your center marker.

1. Approach the circle at a moderate speed.

2. Skate to a point that is 10 feet to the right of your center marker, keeping both knees well bent.

3. Leaning in toward your center marker, begin a glide on the left skate, stroking with the right. Relax the left ankle so the left skate tips onto its outside edge.

4. Recover your right skate to the pavement directly in front of the left, on the perimeter of your circle.

5. Point at your center marker with your right hand, and try to keep facing and looking at it at all times.

6. Gradually try to cross the right skate farther over the left skate as you continue circling. Stop stroking and coast if you find yourself moving too fast for comfort or begin to feel dizzy.

Practice Tips

- Don't worry about how far the outside skate crosses over the inside one for now. Touching down directly in front of the inside skate is an adequate start from which to build.

- Place the inside hand on the back of the hip closest to the center of the circle, with the elbow pointing behind you, not toward the circle's center. If that's too hard, spread your arms wide and imagine you're trying to hug your circle. Keep your gaze fixed on its center.

- Feeling jerky? Still in your circle, shift 3/4 of your weight to the front, left skate and ride on it while swizzling the right skate out and in. On the return from each swizzle, steer the right skate toward the front of the left toe wheel.

- Practice your strong-leg Crossover Turns until you have the mechanics down. Pay attention to what your body is doing. Then start working on the weaker leg and spend twice as much time on it. Don't allow yourself to become a mono-directional skater.

- As you improve, try making Crossovers in progressively smaller circles. Be prepared to handle the speed!

Backward skating

What it is: Backward propulsion by tracing an hour-glass shape on the pavement.
How to learn: Four rolling drills including the 3-part Football Drill and backward turning.

Unless you grew up on ice skates, give yourself time extra to learn how to initiate and maintain backward movement. Don't give up too soon, and remember that once you get the feel of it, you will never forget it.

Before starting any backward skating session, be sure your practice area is entirely clean of debris and free of traffic, since you will not be watching where you are going at all times. In these drills, backward stopping won't be an issue.

BACKWARD TURNS

A backward turn gives you an option for turning out of gravity's pull. This is a nice confidence builder for when you use a slight pitch to learn other backward moves.

Like the basic forward turn, the basic backward turn is built on a sturdy A-fame foundation, and includes the same principals of pressuring and upper body rotation. Tackle your first backward turns on a slight parking lot drainage slope.

1. Standing with your back facing down the slope, assume a wide A-frame stance with knees bent.

2. Allow yourself to start rolling backward.

3. Following with your eyes, sweep your right hand behind you at shoulder height until it points down the hill. As you look over your right shoulder, the rotation pressures the right skate's inside edge, resulting in a right turn. (If not, your feet are too close together.)

4. Repeat two or three times, remembering to take advantage of the slope.

5. Swap feet to make left backward turns by looking over your left shoulder, then try alternating left, right, left, right.

Practice Tips
- As your backward turns improve, try to gain the same results on a flat surface, using only your feet and edges.

- Learn to look over the same shoulder as you alternate from turn to turn.

THE FOOTBALL DRILL

By learning to trace a football shape, you experience the dynamics of forward and backward propulsion. Blend the two together and you learn the subtle foot work that puts you in control of both. In this entire 3-part drill, maintain an upright torso no matter what your feet are doing. Warm up with the forward Swizzle on page 75.

Part 1: Forward movement

From a V-Stance with hands on hips, Swizzle forward in a sideways push with equal pressure on both back wheels. If you keep your toes light, your toe wheels will meet in front and stop the forward movement.

Part 2: Backward movement

Start with the A-Stance (toe wheels touching). You want your heels to be light for easy steering when the toe wheels are pressured.

To swizzle backward, push sideways, not back, with equal pressure against both toe wheels. When your heel wheels can meet lightly behind you, you're ready for Part 3.

Part 3: Draw the football

The moment your wheels meet, whether in front or behind you, immediately push them to the side again to reverse directions. You are now seeking a rhythmic back-and-forth rocking movement as you trace the shape of a football on the pavement. The rhythm comes from learning the foot work while maintaining a still center of gravity.

Keep at it for a few minutes to gain the full benefits of the Football Drill. And by the way, this is a fun way to wait for a stoplight to turn green or chat with skate pals, too!

LINKED BACKWARD SWIZZLES

Let's bring Part 2 (backward) of the Football Drill to full fruition. Don't forget to keep watch over your shoulder as you proceed.

1. Start by repeating the Football Drill three or four times to get your posture and feet in gear.

2. Just before your heel wheels meet going backward, pivot on the balls of your feet until you are in an A-Stance.

3. Begin a new side-directed push with your toe wheels. Don't push toward the back or you'll topple forward!

4. Fully recover both skates before each new backward Swizzle. Seek the rhythm and centered feel of the Football Drill.

Practice Tips
If you're having trouble pulling the skates back together under your hips:

- You have too much weight on the rear wheels of your skates; make sure to push off from the A-stance with toes only.

- Your knees are separating too much; try keeping your knee pads touching while you swizzle with just the lower legs.

BACKWARD STROKES (HALF SWIZZLES)

You can achieve the basic backward stroke by linking together a series of half Backward Swizzles. This skill is best learned on a very slight parking lot drainage slope.

1. With your back to the slope, begin a series of linked Backward Swizzles and get into the swizzle rhythm.

2. At the moment of your narrowest A-Stance, start a sideways push against the toe wheel of the left skate to begin a Half Swizzle. The left skate begins its arc out to the side while the right one rolls straight backward.

3. As the left skate comes back under your left hip, shift your weight over it and begin to press the right skate's toe wheel into a Half Swizzle.

Continue practicing until you can get a short glide from each Half Swizzle. Make sure you keep both skates in constant contact with the ground.

Practice Tips
If you just can't get any momentum:

- Broadly "wag" your hips from side to side to force the weight shift.

- Begin shifting your weight sooner; don't wait for the Swizzling skate get behind you, it must be right under you.

- Return to square one: Use alternating backward turns (see page 88) to force the weight shift. Look over the right shoulder, then twist around to look over the left, then right, then left…

- After you successfully achieve backward momentum, start concentrating on swizzling from the knee down.

Lunge Turns

What it is: A hard swerve at high speed.
How to learn: One stationary, two rolling drills.

Lunge Turns are great in a fast-moving game of hockey or in an emergency. Like Parallel Turns, you must be comfortable moving your upper body outside the axis between your feet. However, in a Lunge Turn your weight distribution is more over the forward skate than with Parallel Turns.

BEFORE YOU ROLL

Warm up with the Crossover drills starting on page 85. The following drill lets you experience the wide, low Lunge Turn stance in a non-rolling situation.

1. Assume the ready position and place your feet in the Safe-T. The right skate serves as both support leg and the top of the T. Raise your hands to waist height within your peripheral vision.

2. Face the same direction as your left toe.

3. Press off the right skate to roll onto the left in a lunge. Keep your chest and shoulders over the left knee.

4. Recover and repeat, upper body forward over the left knee with each lunge.

5. Reverse skates in the Safe-T and practice lunging over the right skate.

A-FRAME TO LUNGE TURN

1. Rolling at a moderate speed, start a left-ward A-frame turn, rotating head, shoulders, hands and hips toward the left.

2. Bend the left knee as you twist and move your upper body toward it.

3. Ride out the turn, and return to a normal, shoulder-width stance.

LUNGE TURN

Use chalk or an object to mark the pavement with an imaginary 90-degree corner.

1. Starting from at least 20 feet away, make a fast approach toward your corner.

2. About 3 feet before you pass your mark, assertively scissors the left skate forward and turn your head and upper body toward the direction of the turn.

3. Sink into a wide, low lunge, making sure to center your chest over the left knee as you transfer most of your weight to that

skate. The trailing leg maintains some
pressure, with the knee slightly bent.

4. Allow centrif-
ugal force to
provide bal-
ance while
both skates
tip onto their
left edges in
the turn.

5. Straighten up
and narrow
the gap
between your
skates to continue rolling in the new
direction.

6. Try to generate enough turning power to
draw a full 180-degree **U** shape on the
pavement with your skates.

Practice Tips
If you do not feel secure over your edges:

• Look over your left shoulder to rotate
your shoulders a quarter turn more than
the hips. Poke your left hip into the circle
of your turn.

• Trust the sticking power of speed plus
centrifugal force; allow your body to tilt
onto the corresponding inside edges.

If your lunge turns feel exactly the same as
your Parallel Turns:

• Put 70% of your weight over the leading
skate and 30% on the trailing skate.
• Separate your skates into a longer stance
and bend both knees more.
• Get your chest out over the leading knee.

Slalom Turns

What it is: Linked turns on corresponding edges.
How to learn: One stationary and four rolling drills.

Slalom Turns are fluid, linked turns wonder-
fully similar to alpine skiing. Besides that
thrill, Slaloms offer speed control on wide
downhills. By "carving" arcs on a slope, you
traverse a lot more of it than you would just
rolling straight down. The long turns and
added friction help keep your speed down.

Although the Slalom Turn uses the pull of
gravity, you can learn it on flat pavement. A
windy day can safely simulate a slope. Just
find a stretch of pavement that forces you to
skate either directly into or away from the

wind. You'll get a good workout skating in one direction and have tons of fun practicing Slalom Turns in the other.

BEFORE YOU ROLL

1. Starting from a ready position, scissors the left skate forward until the ankle is even with the big toe of the right skate.

2. Sink slightly over your feet as you push both knees left to tip your skates onto their left wheel edges.

3. Rise and bring the left foot back under your hips as you simultaneously scissors the right foot ahead.

4. Sink as you push both knees and skates onto the right edges.

5. Repeat several times to experience the rhythm of your future Slalom Turns.

HALF SWIZZLES

Warm up with regular forward Swizzles or the Football Drill.

1. From a moderate speed, begin making forward Swizzles. (See page 75.)

2. At the moment of your narrowest stance, shift your weight to the left skate as you press the right skate's heel wheel outward in a right Half Swizzle. The right skate begins its arc to the side.

3. Once the right skate arcs back under you, shift your weight

onto it and begin to press the left skate into an arc.

4. Continue alternating swizzles, making sure both skates maintain contact with the ground at all times. Try not to rotate your upper body to force a turn; use heel pressure to steer the skates instead.

Practice Tips

- If you have one weak Swizzle leg, do Half Swizzles in a circle, with only the outer foot (the weak leg) stroking. The inside foot simply glides around the circle, supporting most of your weight. Be sure to rotate your head and upper body toward the center of your circle while you pump the outside foot out and in.

TWISTER

This drill loosens your lower body and teaches you how to make tight turns. Do Twisters on flat pavement, not a hill.

1. Stride to gain speed; then begin coasting with arms wide and skates narrow.

2. Without changing your ready position, shift most of your weight onto the back wheels, which lightens the front ones.

3. Still coasting, use knees and ankles to sharply twist both toes right, left, right, left continuously until your speed dissipates. Be sure to keep the heels close together and skates parallel as you "flap" your skates back and forth.

4. Keep your shoulders facing the direction of travel. Go faster to loosen up knees and ankles. Slow loosens the waist and hips (a great variation for snow skiers!).

LINKED PARALLEL TURNS

1. From a moderate speed, start a leftward Parallel turn (see page 78) engaging your left wheel edges.

2. Midturn (skates are 45 degrees across the direction of travel), scissors the right skate forward, switch your weight to the new back skate and make a parallel turn to the right.

3. Continue alternating turns until your speed dissipates, then repeat.

Once you have mastered linked Parallel Turns, you are well on your way to a true Slalom Turn because both of these turns are made on corresponding edges.

SLALOM SKATING

We're almost there! The final touch is to remove the Parallel Turn's upper body rotation. Use the Slalom Turn's "Before you roll" on page 93 as a warm-up drill.

1. Stride to gain a moderate speed.

2. Relax into a coast and then begin to steer both skates into a left turn.

TIPS FOR SKATING IN THE WORLD
When approaching a blind curve on a downhill, slow down, stay to the right, and prepare for a narrow passage. Oncoming skaters will be making wide, climbing strokes and groups of walkers or cyclists may span the width of the trail.

---

3. Sink by bending both knees and tipping them to the left. This increases pressure on your (corresponding) uphill edges and causes a turn. As the turn progresses, your weight naturally transfers to the right skate.

4. Once your skates are both pointing to the left, rise and "uncoil" your bent knees so you can shift most of your weight to the left skate. It now becomes the pressured, **carving** skate (defined on page 17).

5. As your skates straighten out from the left turn, continue steering them into a right turn.

6. Again, sink onto bent knees as you roll both skates onto their uphill edges, initiating the next turn.

7. Practice making both big and small turns to feel the difference in speed reduction. Tighter arcs deliver better speed control.

Tackle the drills in the Advanced Slaloms chapter to refine your expertise or to use Slalom Turns to dramatically (yes, dramatically!) improve your alpine snow skiing.

Stride Three (the power stride)

What it is: Using an enhanced stroke and aerodynamic body position to maximize efficiency.
How to learn: Three stationary drills plus rolling practice for tuck, arm swing and stroke angle.

Stride Three will take you up hills with ease and pave the way for a lifetime of non-impact aerobic workouts. If you have been practicing Stride Two regularly, you should have the balance required to learn this stride's stronger, more efficient stroke. For success at Stride Three you must learn: how to improve your body's aerodynamics; proper use of the arms; correct stride angle and duration; and how to edge when you begin a stroke. The following drills focus on each of these components.

BEFORE YOU ROLL

Aerodynamics
You don't have to be a racer to benefit from a tuck skating position. Lowering your torso even slightly to decrease wind resistance conserves precious energy for a longer workout or a less tiring commute.

1. Standing still with feet shoulder-width apart, fold your hands together, place your knuckles under your chin and touch your elbows to your knees. Notice that even though your head is not right above your hips, in this tuck you are still aligned in a balanced ready position.

2. Now rise a few inches to a similar position that feels comfortable enough to hold while skating. As a balance and weight distribution check, you should be able to hop in place and easily return to this crouch on each landing.

3. Taste the future: Clasp both hands behind your back to experience your ultimate Stride Three tuck form.

Here are some problems and solutions associated with trying to skate in a tuck:

-   **If you don't have the balance** to skate with both hands behind your back, try it with just one arm out of play.

-   **If your lower back starts aching** soon after you begin skating in a tuck, try letting your shoulders and elbows drop with the pull of gravity. This allows your spine to curve downward and relieve some of the stress caused by taut spinal muscles. Try drawing your navel in toward your spine, an opposing contraction that helps release those muscles.

It may take months of practice before you can maintain a tuck for more than a few minutes without experiencing a back ache. Keep at it, and your strength and tolerance will gradually improve.

Arm swing

You may be surprised to learn that the arm swing is front-to-back. One mark of a beginning skater is a side-to-side arm swing that is actually counterproductive to forward momentum. Once you learn an effective Stride Three, you can remove the arm swing altogether. An advanced skater uses a side-to-side swing only for short sprints, up hills or at a race starting line.

1. Standing still, assume your tuck.

2. Starting with both hands at your thighs, palms facing in, swing one hand forward and the other straight back.

3. The back swing straightens out the arm and ends with the little finger pointing up. Simultaneously, the front swing ends with your thumb close to your nose.

4. Begin swinging both arms alternately. With arm swings added to your power stride, the right leg completes a stroke at the same time the left hand's thumb reaches the nose, and vice versa. This should feel as natural as walking.

Stride angle and duration

Do the following while standing with your skates across a painted line or a crack.

1. Standing in your typical skating position, shift your weight to one foot and extend the other skate outward along the line with toes wheels lined up. The extended skate is at your stroke's end.

2. Now assume a deep tuck position. Keeping nose and knee aligned over the support skate's toes, again extend the other

skate along the line. See how much further its path of power is when your support leg is bent at a deeper angle.

3. The painted line reminds you of the proper stroke direction, straight out to the side. For the most power, you must also keep *all* wheels in contact with the pavement throughout the entire length of every stroke: no "toe-flicking"!

QUALITY TIME

Before adding the final component of the power stride, you must get out and incorporate what you've learned so far. Find a location where you can safely skate fast, such as a dedicated bike path during off-peak hours and use the following drills for a few weeks:

• Sets of linked Swizzles (lateral push)
• Alternating Half Swizzles (weight shift)
• Increasing time in a tuck (aerodynamics)
• Arm work (in sprints, tuck, and cruising)

Take a few weeks to get used to your new-found speed and power. You may have balance problems at first, because longer strokes with the action leg result in longer glides with the support leg. To improve stability, spend part of your skate sessions repeating the one-footed balance drills starting on page 81. Spend enough quality time this way, and soon you will be ready to start learning how to use your outside edges to get the most power per stroke.

OUTSIDE EDGE

What it is: Setting recovered skate down on its outside edge to gain maximum stroke length.
How to learn: Four rolling drills.

You can add another inch or two to your already extended stroke by landing your recovered skate a few inches across the **centerline** of travel. With this technique, each stroke begins beyond the centerline on the outside edge, rolls to its center edge as you pull the skate across your centerline, and then pushes into the rest of the stroke with pressure on its inside wheel edges.

Let's take this one element at a time.

Outside Edge Swizzle

To get a feel for using your outside edges to start a stroke, revisit the forward Swizzle (see page 75) with this added twist.

1. Doing forward Swizzles, as your skates reach the narrowest A-Stance, allow your ankles to relax outward so that your skates tip onto their outside edges.

2. After a dozen or so Outside Edge Swizzles in your normal ready position, do several more in a tuck.

3. Return to upright and begin making Half Swizzles (described on page 93).

4. Start each Half Swizzle on the skate's outside edge and roll it over onto the inside edge as you complete the push.

5. Repeat steps 4 and 5 on the opposite leg.

Straddle the centerline

An invisible centerline runs down the middle of a skater's path of travel. With Strides One and Two, it remains between your inside edges. But when you learn Stride Three, the *outside* edge of your recovered skate lands a short way across that line.

This is a rolling drill, but because it's awkward, try the stance at a standstill first.

1. Pass one skate across your centerline and beyond your supporting skate and set it down on the ground 2 or 3 inches away, as if you were starting the Crab Steps drill. Keep both skates parallel.

2. Equalize your weight over your outside edges. Both skates will be tipped under your crossed ankles. Feel where the pressure is inside your boots.

3. Untangle yourself and try the same stance in your tuck position with your hands clasped behind your back.

4. Now coasting forward slowly on the pavement, try rolling on both sets of your outside edges. It's a speedskater's drill: don't feel bad if you fumble at first.

5. Now practice the opposite ankle cross.

Three-edge strokes

1. In your aerodynamic tuck, stride at a moderate pace on a bike path. Imagine you can see your centerline.

2. Begin stroking with just one leg, supporting your weight with the other.

3. Complete several strokes by returning the action skate to the pavement right on top of the centerline.

4. Next, try to land it beyond the centerline before pushing into a stroke.

5. Are you landing on the outside edge? You will experience a small surge of power when you do this correctly.

6. Practice hard on your other foot, too.

Half power strides

It's difficult to determine whether or not you are actually landing on your outside edges, especially without any visual cues (see the line over the photo above). If your local bike path has a painted centerline, that helps, because you can see when you are setting a skate down beyond it while your head and center of gravity stay centered above it.

Regardless of the visual cues, it's easier to learn Stride Three with one foot at a time.

1. Skating in your best form, use the arm swing, long strokes and a tuck. Build up to your highest comfortable speed so the force of each stroke puts you into optimal position for your set down goal.

2. Once you're in good rhythm, begin landing just one skate on its outside edge beyond the centerline; this is a one-sided Stride Three. With the other leg, continue to stroke using Stride Two.

3. Feel pressure along the outside edge of your Stride Three foot each time that skate hits the pavement; feel the short pull as it rolls from its outside to its inside wheel edges and begins a push.

4. Once you can consistently achieve this feedback on one side, switch the Stride Three focus to the opposite leg.

5. Finally, build up to a full power stride by initiating all strokes from an outside edge landed beyond the centerline. This is Stride Three. Isn't it fun to go fast!

PUTTING IT ALL TOGETHER

Put all of the Stride Three components together whenever you can skate fast without fear of harming yourself or others. With dedicated practice, your power stride will deliver not only speed and grace, but a top-notch workout as well.

180-degree transitions

What it is: Rotating from front to back or from back to front while rolling.
How to learn: Four rolling drills.

Now that you can skate backward, you need to learn how to transition smoothly from forward to backward motion and vice versa.

FORWARD-TO-BACKWARD MOHAWK

You can switch from forward to backward skating by building on the Spin Stop you learned in the Beginning Skills chapter.

backward skating exit

spin and pivot

foreward skating entry

1. Skating at a moderate speed, begin a counterclockwise Spin Stop (page 76.)

2. As soon as your left heel wheel returns to the pavement, shift your weight onto the left skate.

3. Pivot quickly on the right skate's toe wheel to make that skate parallel with the left as your hips finish rotating to the backward position. This leaves you rolling backward with both skates parallel.

4. Complete the transition by pushing off into your favorite backward movement.

BACKWARD-TO-FORWARD BASIC TRANSITION

This version of the backward-to-forward 180-degree transition is much easier than you might think because it originates from the backward turn you already know. Learn this skill on your parking lot drainage slope.

1. Allow yourself to start rolling backward.

2. Begin a backward turn by looking over your right shoulder.

3. When you have rotated a quarter turn (hips are perpendicular to the direction of travel), briefly shift your weight to the uphill (left) skate.

4. With your weight on the left leg, and your body already halfway rotated, it's easy to lift and finish rotating your right skate to point it downhill.

5. The moment the right skate touches down, utilize the pressure still on the left skate to push smoothly off into a forward glide. Try it, you'll like it!

If you have trouble getting both feet turned around, imagine that your skates are as big as clown shoes. You must pick up one of these great big feet and swing it all the way around until it is pointing forward before you put it back down on the pavement. In the drill above, that would be the right skate.

FORWARD-TO-BACKWARD PIVOT

Learn both Forward-to-Backward and Backward-to-Forward Pivots using raised arms as rotation guides. Eliminate this aid when it is no longer useful. Try this transition standing still first and then repeat at a roll. Start from a solid ready position with knees well bent.

1. Raise both outstretched hands to shoulder height. Position the left hand pointing straight ahead and the right pointing directly behind. Your arms are now lined up with the (future) direction of travel.

2. Fixing your gaze on the left hand, raise both heels no more than an inch off the pavement and swing both hips and heels clockwise, pivoting on the front toe wheels 180 degrees.

3. Return the heels to the pavement. You are now looking "backward" over your left shoulder; however, eyes remained fixed on the left hand, which does not move during the entire movement.

4. Now try it while rolling slowly along a straight line on smooth, flat pavement. Start from a slow coast, rolling forward toward your raised left hand.

For best results, keep your knees bent and your upper body movements smooth as you rotate the lower body.

BACKWARD-TO-FORWARD PIVOT

Try this transition standing still first.

1. Raise both outstretched hands to shoulder height with the left hand pointing straight ahead and the right pointing directly behind. Again, your arms are lined up with the direction of travel.

2. Without moving the positions of your arms, look over your shoulder at your right hand. This is the starting position when you are skating backward and want to change to forward.

3. Eyes fixed on the right hand, pivot on both skates' heel wheels to rotate hips, knees and toes clockwise 180 degrees.

4. Return toes to the pavement. Head and hands do not move during the entire

movement; arms remain lined up in the direction of travel.

5. Now try the same thing while rolling along a straight line on smooth, flat pavement. Start from a slow coast, rolling backward and looking at your raised right hand or an object beyond it.

Bent knees and a quiet upper body keep the action smooth as you rotate the lower body.

Advanced stops and slowing techniques

ONE-FOOTED HEEL BRAKING

What it is: Transferring full weight to the heel brake.
How to learn: One drill.

As an intermediate skater, your increased confidence and better balance and stroking technique allow you to skate faster than when you first started out. Since the distance required to stop increases in proportion to your speed, you absolutely must know how to maximize that heel brake. This is done by transferring your weight forward from the support leg to the heel brake itself.

Practicing the following drill will do wonders for your high speed stopping capabilities. And, yes, it's a great way to impress your friends! (This is much easier to do with plastic than with soft boots, by the way.)

Warm up by practicing the Training Wheel drill (see page 82) and Stopping on a Line (page 72) in the Beginning Skills chapter.

1. At a moderate speed, relax into a coasting ready position.

2. Pick up your left heel and press your left front wheel firmly down about 6 inches behind your right skate's back wheel. Maintain a narrow, parallel stance.

3. Scissors the right skate forward and engage the heel brake forcefully, pushing forward, not down.

4. Roll to a stop, then return all eight wheels to the pavement immediately to prevent loss of balance. Repeat until you can do this with stability and confidence.

5. Now work on actually raising your rear skate off the pavement entirely. (See

photo.) You don't have to start from the Training Wheel position to practice this.

T-STOP
What it is: Stopping by dragging your wheels.
How to learn: One stationary, two rolling drills.

If you have good one-footed balance, you are ready to try the T-Stop. Be aware that relying on this as your only stopping method can use up perfectly good wheels in a hurry. A heel brake is cheaper to replace and is more effective tool when stopping really counts. If you already have knee problems, I strongly recommend you stick with the heel brake.

In the following drills, rather than referring to the left and right skate, the support leg is the one that bears your weight, and the action leg is the one handling the braking activity (as defined in "Key Terms" on page 17.) This gives you more flexibility in learning, which is especially useful when you aren't really sure which leg is the best to perform which role. This is that kind of skill.

Before you roll
Start by warming up with some of the one-footed balance drills described in the Beginning Skills chapter. Then, prepare yourself for the T-Stop by experiencing its components one at a time. You may have better luck doing this drill twice, once on the lawn where you won't roll, and once standing still on the pavement.

1. Starting from the ready position with your hands at waist level and within

view, shift and center all of your weight onto the support foot.

2. In one quick motion, lift the action leg just enough to flip the skate outward 90 degrees and return it to the ground directly behind and perpendicular to the supporting leg's skate. Throughout the movement, maintain a fixed upper body position, facing forward.

3. Practice making this quick flip several times to familiarize your muscles with the proper degree of rotation required to get the braking skate perpendicular to the support leg's skate. Work for speed and accuracy; both will be welcome once you do this in motion.

4. Continue flipping the braking skate, but change your focus to the touchdown. All wheels must touch the pavement at the same time, or you may end up making a spin stop or tripping yourself.

5. In the T-Stop position, tuck your pubic bone forward and press down with the action skate. This movement helps you add braking pressure from the inside of the foot without overly stressing the action leg's knee joint.

T-Drag

The T-Drag allows you to bring together all components of the T-Stop except the actual stop. This is a skill in its own right, commonly used by brakeless folk for speed reduction.

1. Assume a coasting ready position at a moderate speed.

2. Shift your weight over your support leg.

3. Lift and rotate the action skate a full 90 degrees, moving it into T position behind the support skate's heel.

4. Maintaining a solid forward-facing upper body position, carefully touch all wheels onto the pavement at the same time. Don't worry about how much gap there is between the braking skate and the support skate.

5. Repeat the T-Drag several times on your strong leg and try it at least once on the opposite leg, just to make sure you're working on the best one for you.

T-Stop

1. Repeat steps 1-5 of the T-Drag. This is your T-Stop approach.

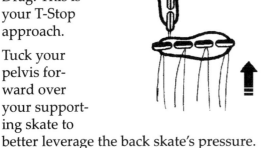

2. Tuck your pelvis forward over your supporting skate to better leverage the back skate's pressure.

3. Gradually increase the pressure on the dragging wheels by pulling the action skate closer to the support skate.

4. Repeat the T-Stop at progressively faster speeds while attempting to shorten the distance it takes to stop. For best results, practice stopping on a line.

Practice Tips

- **If you find yourself going into a spin**, try harder to touch all of the wheels down at the same time, and work on keeping the upper body and hands facing squarely forward throughout the movement.

- **If this hurts your knee**, concentrate on tucking your pelvis forward by rounding your lower back. As a less knee-stressing alternative, ease into the T-Stop by starting the drag from more of a V-Stance instead of perpendicular. The wheels roll a little as you drag, which saves wear on their edges.

BACKWARD POWER SLIDE

What it is: A lunge stop going backwards.
How to learn: One rolling drill.

The Backward Power Slide is used for stopping when skating backward. When done correctly, this move ends in a lunge with the braking skate extended in the direction of travel, low on its inside wheel edges.

Before attempting this Power Slide variation (there are others, but not in these pages), warm up by practicing your backward turns (page 88) and backward strokes (page 90). This drill uses the left leg as the support leg and the right leg as the action (braking) leg.

1. Starting with your favorite backward skating method, relax into a moderate-paced coast. Look over your right shoulder and spot an object or mark on the pavement 15 feet in the direction of travel.

2. Sink deeply over the left, front knee and begin to arc the right skate out to the side and back, at the same time transferring pressure to its inside wheel edges.

3. Begin to rise slightly from over the left leg so that you can increase the pressure on the right skate's inside edges. Reach maximum pressure just before the right skate crosses between you and the mark on the pavement. This friction is what causes you to stop.

See the finishing body position in the drawing on the next page. This skater's direction of travel is toward his right, extended (braking) skate.

1. Skating at a moderate speed, fix your eyes on an object or mark on the pavement 15 feet ahead.

2. Begin a Lunge Turn toward the left without looking away from the mark.

3. Leaning over the left knee, begin to arc the right skate into the turn. As it swings around, begin transferring pressure from your left side onto the sharply angled wheels of the right skate.

4. Apply the maximum pressure to your right skate's inside wheel edges just before it crosses between you and the mark on the pavement. To do so, rise slightly from the lunge, which adds stopping friction. In a nutshell, go in low and come out high.

5. Keep practicing. Remember, hips and shoulders are facing the direction of travel to begin; at finish they are rotated 90 degrees to the left.

Practice Tips

- **If you find yourself making A-frame Turns** instead of stopping with your Lunge Stops, you are not lowering your upper body into the lunge turn position before transferring pressure to the trailing skate's inside wheel edges.

- **If you cannot interrupt the Lunge Turn** to force a stop, you are not transferring your weight from the support leg to the action skate's angled wheels. To correct this, be sure to keep your eyes fixed on an object in the direction of travel beyond your intended stopping point.

Practice Tips

- For better balance throughout the maneuver, keep your eyes on your mark.

- Hips and shoulders are facing away from the direction of travel to begin, and finish rotated 90 degrees to the right.

- Go in low and come out high.

LUNGE STOP

What it is: A hard, wide swerve into a lunge that uses the friction of one skate s wheel edges to stop.
How to learn: One rolling drill.

The Lunge Stop is an aggressive way to terminate fast forward momentum, and is used extensively in roller hockey. (The "Hockey Stop," a similar stop made on corresponding edges, is possible with lots of practice but is outside the scope of this book.) Warm up with Spin Stops (page 76) and Lunge Turns (page 91) before you begin the drill.

SNOW PLOW

What it is: Slowing down with a big, hard Swizzle.
How to learn: One rolling drill.

The Snow plow is useful for slowing (if not stopping) those who skate brakeless, serving as an alternative or final touch for the T-Stop on relatively flat ground. It is based on a speed reduction skill used by beginning snow skiers, where the skis form a wide wedge shape.

1. Start making forward Swizzles at a moderate pace.

2. Apply pressure to both inside edges just as your toes steer inward. Use your hip muscles to increase the pressure.

3. If your toes seem destined to meet soon, swizzle them out and begin another Snow plow.

4. Practice stopping on a line to learn your capabilities in a real-world situation.

As you get stronger, you may have better results by tipping your skates *outward*. When you engage your outside edges you can supplement the pressure and your braking leverage with outer hip muscles.

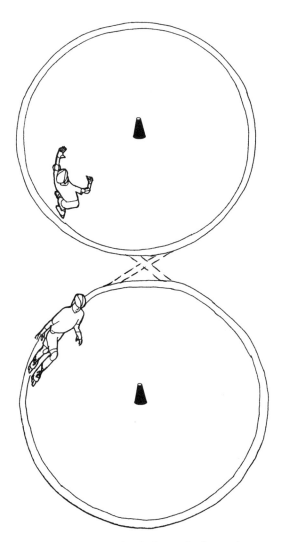

Mobility and balance drills

What it is: More fast-track drills for skating success.
How to learn: Three turning and one backwards drill, plus three drills to learn Backward Crossovers.

FIGURE EIGHTS

You can strengthen both directions of your forward Crossover Turns (without getting dizzy!) by skating in big figure eights.

At a school yard, look for side-by-side painted circles, about 15 feet in diameter. If such a location is not available, go to your favorite empty parking lot and place two cones or other markers on the pavement about 30 feet apart, and imagine a circle around each, forming a figure eight.

1. Begin skating Crossover Turns in a counterclockwise lap around one of the circles. Focus your eyes on the circle's center and rotate your shoulders and hips toward the center.

2. At the end of a lap near the second circle, make one or two regular forward glides onto it and turn your head to the right to look at the second circle's center.

3. Begin making clockwise Crossover Turns, this time with your upper body rotated to the right toward the center of the second circle.

4. Continue. At first, take two laps around each circle before changing directions, then begin making a full figure eight each lap.

ALTERNATING CROSSOVERS

This is a rhythmic and fun movement that you can use for exercise, climbing hills, or as a variation of the regular forward glide. Because of its zigzag path, it requires a swath of pavement at least 15 feet wide, such as a parking lot or one lane of an unused street. This may look complicated on paper, but you are simply inserting one crossover after every two forward glides. Make it a point to rehearse these motions on carpet or lawn first.

1. Stride to gain a moderate speed alongside the left edge of your wide path.

2. From a glide on the right foot, allow your upper body to shift further to the right, passing the left foot over the right.

3. Complete the Crossover by placing the left skate on the pavement to the right of the right skate.

4. Retrieve the right skate and push off into a right glide. That was the "zig."

5. To "zag," begin a glide on the left skate. This stride changes your direction of travel toward the left.

6. Allow your upper body to pass further to the left, and perform a Crossover.

7. Follow the Crossover with a left and then a right glide.

8. Continue the sequence as long as you have the room. The rhythm is: right-glide, Crossover, right-glide; left-glide, Crossover, left-glide.

TURN ON A LINE

In this parking lot drill, you use painted parking space lines to trigger alternating forward-to-backward and backward-to-forward transitions of any type (see the drills starting on page 98). To aid in spotting, you will keep your eyes fixed on the far end (the

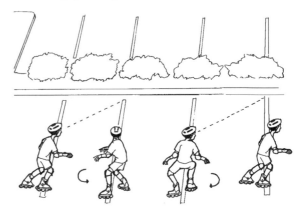

head) of the parking space line as you make 180-degree turns over the tail end of the line. Find a series of at least ten empty parking spaces.

1. With a long row of painted parking space lines ahead and to your left, begin skating.

2. Visually spot the end of a line two parking spaces ahead of you. Keep your eyes there as you perform the following sequence.

3. Just as you are about to cross your spotting line, perform a *counter-clockwise* forward-to-reverse turn toward the head of the line.

4. Continue to skate backward across two or more parking spaces. Looking over your right shoulder, spot a new line further up your row of parking spaces.

5. At the new line, make a *clockwise* backward-to-forward turn toward the head end of the line.

6. Repeat the sequence of 180-degree transitions until you run out of parking spaces.

7. Repeat this drill as you head back toward your starting point; this time you will be practicing your *clockwise* forward-to-backward turns and *counter-clockwise* backward-to-forward turns.

8. Once you're successful using the parking space lines as spotting aids, begin practicing without spotting.

This drill is worth much repetition, because it results in smooth and confident 180-degree transitions at varying speeds in any direction.

BACKWARD PLAY

Here are some fun ways to improve balance and confidence for backward skating. Find a clean, traffic-free area so you don't have to worry about what's behind you.

- Practice starting backward from a standstill using linked backward Swizzles. See if you can start and continue to skate backward up a slight slope. When you can do this, you've really got it!

- Build some backwards momentum and then relax into a coast. Try the Marching Drill (page 83) going backwards. This can do wonders for your balance, (but check behind you frequently to be sure your path is clear!).

BACKWARD CROSSOVERS

Backward Crossovers do not come easily to most skaters, but fortunately this skill isn't required to get around or have fun. (However, you'll want to master it if you're interested in figure skating or roller hockey.) Simply attempting this skill helps improve your overall balance and mobility.

Before you roll

Warm up with a series of leftward Crab Steps (page 63) and then do the following.

1. Starting from a well-flexed ready position (the deeper your knees are bent the better), stretch both arms out to the side

and twist your upper body to the left until the right arm is pointing across your body and the left arm is pointing directly behind you.

2. Rotate your head until your chin is nearly over your left shoulder. (Fortunately, you will be facing the direction of travel in this twisted position.)

3. Next, shift all of your weight to the left skate and then scissors the right skate ahead so that the heel wheel is directly lined up with the left skate's toe wheel. Flex your knees a few times to experience these new balance demands.

4. Maintaining the upper body rotation and balance over your left skate, reposition the right skate 3-5 inches to the left, beyond the left skate's toe. Keeping it scissored ahead, try moving it from side to side, simulating the swizzling motion you will use for propulsion. In the actual Crossover, this skate does not leave the pavement.

Circling Half Swizzles
Find a large open area free of debris and traffic. This drill is best performed on the edge of a painted game circle such as those found in school yards.

1. Begin making Backward Swizzles clockwise around the circle, checking your path over your left shoulder.

2. Transfer most of your weight over your left knee and continue the in-and-out motion with just your right skate. This keeps you skating around the circle.

3. Bend your knees, outstretch both arms, and then twist to the left, toward the center of the circle. This helps you to transfer your weight to the outside edge of the left skate—this is the scary part!

4. Try to sweep the Swizzling skate ahead of the support skate and further inside the circle with each stroke.

5. Continue making Half Swizzles in a circle, maintaining steady balance over the support leg while swizzling the right skate to supply backward propulsion.

Crossovers
1. Start with Circling Half Swizzles, skating backwards in a clockwise circle.

2. Allow the left skate's ankle to relax so that it tips onto its outside edge. This should be a natural result when you get your upper body fully rotated toward the center of the circle.

3. Allow the left skate to pass underneath your body and away from the center of the circle, all the while tipped onto its outside edge. As it crosses under your hips and you begin to feel as though you haven't a leg to stand on (literally!)…

4. … swizzle the right skate forward inside the perimeter of the circle so it can take your weight.

5. With thighs now crossed, begin to push the right skate back out. Recover the left skate from afar and return it to the pavement directly under your left hip. (This recovery is the only time either skate leaves the ground.)

6. Continue making Crossovers in a circle. You'll achieve best results by remembering to maintain well-bent knees and good upper body rotation.

This skill builds speed. Switch to regular backward Swizzles or do a 180-degree transition to forward skating if you need to slow down or stop. Or maybe you'd like to use your backward Lunge stop or backward Power Slide?

Practice Tip
Hockey players practice a Backward Crossover version on a long, straight stretch of pavement rather than on a circle. While the action skate snakes repeatedly in and out, the support skate rides on its center edges instead of being tipped onto the outside wheel edges. Without pressure on either side edge, there is no turn. That makes this form of backwards Crossovers another form of backward skating.

Handling urban obstacles

What it is: What you find in the real world.
How to learn: Dealing with curbs and common obstacles on the trail and street, and getting air!

TAKING CURBS AT A ROLL

Eventually, you'll want to be able deal with curbs while in motion. If you feel uncomfortable rolling on one foot, go back and practice the one-footed balance drills described in the Beginning Skills chapter (starting on page 81).

Whether going up or down, approach curbs at an angle to reduce the distance you must step across. And don't approach too slowly, or you will lose your stability.

1. **Getting up**: A foot out from the curb, lift one skate high enough to clear it, while reaching over the curb with both arms. As you step onto the higher pavement, push off against the inside wheel edges of the support leg below to keep your momentum.

2. **Stepping off**: As you near the curb, lean over it and reach forward with both arms while lifting and extending the action skate far enough ahead to clear the edge. (Be sure to leave plenty of clearance if you're stepping off with the brake skate first.) Land this skate at an angle that will allow you to push off into a glide as soon as you recover the other skate.

3. **Rolling off:** If you aren't at a busy intersection and no cars are in sight, you can simply relax and roll straight off the curb at skating speed with both skates paral-

lel. There's no need to hop or jump: as long as you maintain that ever-lovin' ready position, you will drop lightly to the pavement and continue rolling along at the same momentum. If you're worried about your brake catching on the curb, scissors that skate ahead slightly and increase your approach speed.

HOP-OVERS

Practice the Hop-Over drills that follow, and soon you will have the confidence to hop onto most of the curbs in your path. This skill is a must for the budding aggressive skater.

You want to practice by doing a stationary hop on the grass first, before progressing to a stationary hop on the pavement.

Warning: Most of us are used to using our toes to jump. However, to avoid crashes when learning hop-overs, be careful not to push off with your toes or heels. Since your foot is fixed to a flat, inflexible frame, hopping while on skates requires a *flat-footed* launch (thus the impending doom faced by the youngster in this drawing!)

> **TIPS FOR SKATING IN THE WORLD**
> If you can see a rock in the trail from 20 feet away, avoid it. On the other hand, anything that isn't immediately obvious from that distance will most likely just pop out from under your wheels if you roll right over it.

1. Assume your best ready position with hands just below waist level.

2. Starting from flexed knees, spring up 1 to 2 inches off the ground. You don't need to reach for the stars, but a slight lift of the hands helps with balance.

3. Land on flat feet. Let your legs absorb the impact as you land. The key to keeping your balance is to maintain that solid ready position.

4. Now let's get rolling. To help focus your effort, choose a line, crack or other mark on the pavement to hop over. Approach your Grand Canyon coasting at a moderate speed in your best ready position.

5. Lightly spring 1 to 2 inches off the ground and then allow your legs to absorb the impact as you land. Try not to swing your arms wildly, or you'll crash.

6. Continue to practice hopping over lines and cracks in your practice area, working on good body position throughout the jump and landing.

7. Once you're King or Queen of the Cracks, try leaping higher and tucking your heels up under your hips. Success

with this can be construed as proof that you are ready to hop up your first curb.

OTHER COMMON OBSTACLES

As your skills and confidence improve, you will acquire a broadening perspective on where you can go on in-line skates. Relish this, but remember, skating terrain is full of challenges besides curbs—other obstacles, changes in surfaces, and stairs. Here are tips for handling a variety of unforeseen elements skaters face every day.

Manhole covers and cattle guards

These are city and country versions of a similar physical hurdle to skaters. Avoid them if you can, just as you would a pothole or patch of gravel. If you approach with enough speed, you can roll right over most manhole covers in a solid scissors position. When you encounter cattle guards (real, not painted ones) step or—if you're really a pro—leap over them. Learn to stay on the alert for such obstacles and enjoy the challenge of dealing with them.

Slick spots, wet leaves, and puddles

In-line wheel traction can almost disappear on slick surfaces. Avoid them if you can. For long, unavoidable wet patches, build up your speed before you hit them so you can coast all the way across without having to stroke. Consider riding on one skate so you'll only have to wipe dry half your wheels to prevent rusted bearings.

If you get caught in the rain or find yourself skating across a really large patch of oil, water, or wet leaves, take shorter, light-pressure strokes and stay centered over your feet. This is where Stride One really shines! (See page 64.)

Steep hills

There is one sure-fire way to get safely down any decline: dare to be a "wimp"! Simply take your skates off and walk when a hill looks too steep for your heel brake or speed-control skills. Don't even consider rolling it out and hoping for the best. Besides increased chances for intimate contact with a moving vehicle, just hitting a pebble the wrong way at high speed can cause a serious accident, too. If it's a short slope, you might try side stepping down: Face across the hill and step sideways until you reach the bottom. If you're lucky enough to have a railing, use it. If there is grass or soft dirt near the path, step down that.

Wooden bridges

The faster you skate over a bumpy wooden bridge, the easier it will be to get across and keep your balance. To deal with the same problem as you climb an arched bridge, take short, quick Stride One strokes with toes out and your weight forward. On the downhill part of an arch, just relax and roll in a scissored stance, keeping your body as loose and centered over your feet as possible.

Stairs

Accomplished street skaters can do some amazing stunts with stairs, including riding them forward, backward, or with knees pointing both fore and aft. Sorry, folks, but such stunts are not described in *Get Rolling*.

At first, it is easier to both ascend and descend stairs by facing toward them. As your balance improves, you will be able to walk down stairs facing the normal direction. Handle stairs as though they were a series of multiple curbs and avoid stairs without railings unless you're confident you can handle them.

1. **To ascend a flight of stairs,** grip the railing (if available), and place a skate on the first step with the front wheel rolled up against the side at a toe-out angle.

2. Lean forward as you transfer your weight to the upstairs skate and...

3. ... place the second skate on the second step, toes angled out, and rolled up against the side of the next step.

4. Focus on leaning forward as you climb. This helps lock your front wheels into the side of the stairs.

1. **To descend stairs**, grip the railing (use both hands if it feels better) and extend your right skate down the first step.

2. Roll your back wheel against the wall of the step, toes angled toward the railing.

3. Using the railing for support, bring the left skate down, either to the same step (both skates will be parallel and angled toward the railing) or, if you feel com-

> ### TIPS FOR SKATING IN THE WORLD
> Practice hops and long jumps often. These skills come in handy when unexpected obstacles or debris lie across your path.

fortable, to the next step down. Set it down angled toward the railing.

4. Make your way down the stairs.

If you are worried about descending the stairs facing forward, turn around and do it backward. Simply reverse the ascending instructions and use the railing for support. If there is no railing and there are lots of stairs, play it safe by removing your skates altogether.

Tricks to impress your friends

JUMP TURNS

Here's how to make hot-looking forward-to-backward and backward-to-forward turns by rotating 180 degrees in midair.

Warm up by practicing Hop-Overs as described on page 110. Then, go to a dry patch of lawn and practice jumping up and turning halfway around before landing (start with your favorite direction). Lead by rotating your head first.

When you feel confident with 180s on the lawn, go back to the pavement and try some low Jump Turns from a complete standstill. When you're finally ready to roll, try your first Jump Turns with the Turn on a Line drill described on page 106 so you can use the parking space lines as spotting aids.

Repeat the same movements you used on the grass to hop just high enough rotate your hips, knees and skates 180 degrees counterclockwise.

HEEL-TOE ROLL

To do the Heel-Toe Roll, you must have only one heel brake attached. The following instructions assume the brake is on the right skate. Practice the Training Wheel drill described on page 82 as a warm-up.

1. Begin coasting at a moderate pace with your feet shoulder-width apart.

2. Pick up your right heel and allow your right toe wheel to bear about half of your

body weight as it rolls 3 to 6 inches behind your left heel.

3. In one quick movement, push your left skate ahead of you. As your left knee straightens out, the left toe lifts off the pavement so that you are rolling on just one back wheel (it may help to throw your hands up to the sides to briefly lighten the load on your feet).

4. Now you are rolling forward on the right toe wheel and the left heel wheel in a wide scissors position.

5. For variety, see how far you can spread your skates apart and how low you can get to the ground (this may depend more on flexibility than skill).

DOUBLE TOE ROLL

Once you've got the Heel-Toe roll, you're ready to try rolling on both toe wheels at the same time. This looks pretty flashy going forward, and the Double Toe roll is even more impressive when you can do it going backwards.

1. Begin coasting at a moderate pace with your feet shoulder-width apart.

2. Pick up your right heel and allow your right toe wheel to bear about

half of your body weight as it rolls 3 to 6 inches behind your left heel.

3. Sink a few inches to flex your left knee.

4. Raise the left heel as high off the pavement as possible. The higher both heels are, the flashier the trick. Flexed knees allow the heels to lift higher.

SIDE SURFING

Spin Stops can be turned into full 360-degree turns. Once both skates are in the turned-out position, a wide, knees-out squat results in a large radius spin or a first attempt at Side Surfing. A true Side Surf—skating heels-in and toes-out, going forward instead of in a circle—requires very flexible hip joints.

1. Start by initiating a Spin Stop on the right skate's inside edge. This will make you turn to the left, counterclockwise.

2. Lift the left skate's heel and pivot on the toe wheel so you are skating heel to heel.

3. The moment your heel returns to the pavement, equalize your weight over both skates.

4. Keep feet wide apart and squat deeply to Side Surf in a circle until the momentum dies.

For a true Side Surf, you must put your left skate down on its outside edge in step two, then lean your upper body slightly backward, with knees bent at nearly 90 degrees.

GET ROLL'N

Intermediate Skills

CHAPTER 6

Advanced Slaloms

In-line skating is so complementary to skiing that many professional alpine skiers skate for cross training in the dry months. Recreational skiers, too, improve their skills whenever they skate "carved" turns down hills. Downhill expertise is built on good one-footed balance, excellent heel-braking abilities, and the wherewithal to maintain a rock-solid composure at speeds in the upper range of your comfort zone.

Whether you're on snow or asphalt, you can't learn expert slalom skills in a day. And for you skiers, the yodel-inspiring benefits of centered balance over effortlessly turning skis will only begin to blossom after you can perform proper, corresponding-edge Slalom Turns on your in-lines.

The lessons in this chapter begin by focusing on the large muscles and movements of the lower body, and then help you refine your technique through arm use.

You can practice the drills with or without a slalom course. Although a row of cones isn't necessary when first learning these moves, consider using them later on, because a slalom course forces you to learn better timing and control.

Before plunging right into the lessons in this chapter, it's important you understand safety and survival on big hills. Remember, no hill initially *looks* as big as it is going to feel once gravity begins its eager pull!

Dealing with speed

If you can only remember only one piece of advice in this book, make it this one: avoid reaching "terminal velocity"—anticipate speed buildup and begin your slowing maneuvers *before* you get out of control and have to dive to stop. An intermittent application of the heel brake or a T-drag should do the trick. If not, the hill is too steep for skating (or you need to work on these skills). Know your own speed comfort zone, and choose your practice hills accordingly.

At velocities of 30 or more miles per hour, the heel brake has been proven again and again to be the best speed reducer because it's the easiest to engage with the least risk for loss of balance. Heel brakes also cause less muscle fatigue when applied over a long distance, and require less distance than all other (non-crashing) methods to reach a complete stop. Cuff-activated braking systems are favored by avid downhillers because the brake can be engaged with all eight wheels in contact with the pavement, resulting in better balance and less interruption to the joy of linked slaloms.

Purchase heel-brake replacement pads three at a time so that you always have a backup after (or in the middle of) a thrilling day of downhills.

Location tips

You can gain the benefits of the following drills on a slope that is barely discernible. However, the best place to learn advanced Slalom techniques is on an empty, gently sloped street with a long, flat run-out at the bottom. Drive around your local ritzy neighborhood to find the best street with the least traffic. Progress very gradually to steeper hills as your skills improve.

Test your hill. Roll forward for 10 feet and then terminate the roll with a Heel-brake Stop. If you can't, this hill is too steep for you to learn to slalom. If your slope seems too intimidating or steep from the top, walk or drive to the bottom, skate partway up, and

---

TIPS FOR SKATING IN THE WORLD
Plan ahead for hilly routes: Carry a fresh heel brake and unrocker your wheels for better stability at high speeds.

---

start from there to give yourself a shorter hill. As you get more capable and confident, skate back up a bit farther for each run. Soon, you'll find you can start at the top.

Lower body control

SINK AND RISE

As your lower leg tilts around to arc into a Slalom Turn, centrifugal force builds up in the form of pressure under the wheels. This drill teaches you how to take advantage of these forces to gain better speed control. Warm up with the Slalom Skating drill from the Intermediate Skills chapter (see page 92).

1. Slalom down your hill. To sink at the bottom of each turn, increase pressure on the downhill skate by bending your knees with chest upright. Keep your pelvis tucked slightly forward and let your hips drop toward your downhill heel, adding centered pressure from above.

2. At the moment of greatest pressure, straighten your knees slightly so you can easily transfer your weight onto the uphill skate, initiating a new turn, then

3. Now bend your knees and drop your hips to sink into the next turn.

4. Finish each turn in a sink and start the next one with a rise. Make sure you do not bend at the waist to do this—stack your skeleton directly over your hips and heels.

TIPS FOR TIGHT TURNS

On steeper hills, you'll need to shorten your turns to maintain adequate speed control. The more turns you can make to press those edges into the pavement, the less velocity you build. Learning to make shorter turns will also give you better skating agility. Each of the following tips assumes you have started making slalom turns from the top of your practice hill. Keep your knees well bent to get the most from the following tips.

- Just after you shift your weight to initiate a new turn, push the weighted skate's knee forward and inward to help steer your skate in the direction of the turn.

- For better tight turn maneuverability, rocker your wheels if your skate model offers that feature. (See "Rockering the wheels" on page 44 in the Avoiding Injuries chapter for instructions).

- When your turning skate arcs around in front of you, make a deliberate punch on the heel of that skate to finish the turn. Be sure you push the heel straight down rather than away from you, using your hamstrings and buttocks muscles. Besides adding extra friction to slow you down, the recoil from the punch helps propel your upper body to the proper position for starting the next turn.

• For the tightest turns, keep your upper body facing squarely toward the bottom of the hill while your lower body does all the rotating, as shown in the photo above.

• To initiate a new turn, transfer your weight from the carving skate onto the front two wheels of the new turning skate while it is still uphill of the turn, asserting control from the very start. As the skate enters the turn, rock the pressure back to the rear wheels so that you can add the finishing punch from the heel of the skate.

ONE-FOOTED CARVES

If you allow your skates to roll unchecked during the transition between each Slalom, you will find it more and more difficult to maintain a comfortable speed descending a long hill. As soon as the turning skate takes your weight, however, it can begin edging to cut speed. The following drill focuses on turn timing, so you are aware of the moment you can begin to edge. It's also a way to learn about independent footwork and, as such, is a great balance drill. One-Footed Carving is one of the best ski cross training exercises because it forces the body to stay centered over the carving edge and reduces the tendency to shove the turning leg downhill in order to "put on the brakes."

1. Start rolling down your practice hill.

2. At the moment you transfer your weight to the uphill skate to start a new turn, lift the lower skate an inch off the pavement.

3. Sink into the turn, riding the arc on just the one skate until it crosses the fall line.

4. As you finish the carve with a slight push on the heel, the knee straightens, causing you to rise from your compressed position.

TIPS FOR SKATING IN THE WORLD
When using hard-carving turns on a downhill slope, plan ahead to avoid hitting maximum edging pressure on a painted crosswalk line, wet leaves or a damp patch, where sudden slickness can send you crashing to the pavement.

---

5. Transfer your weight onto the new uphill skate at the same moment you raise the other just off the pavement. The weight-shift movement should feel similar to pedaling a bicycle half a crank. Sink into your next turn.

6. Make large, One-Footed Carves all the way down your hill. Develop your awareness and muscle memory of the timing of that pedaling weight shift. Skiers, this is also the moment of pole plant.

7. For good measure, at the bottom of your hill make the turnaround to skate back uphill a One-Footed Carve on your bad side. Do this often enough, and you'll no longer have a bad side!

Separating upper from lower body

Now that you know what to do with your lower body, you need to loosen up your midsection to allow your upper body to remain quiet and centered in spite of all that action going on below. Here's a drill that teaches you stay low and loose. (And it's just the trick for skiers who want to improve their mogul runs.) You need a sloped parking lot with a fall line that lets you slalom the tail ends of the painted parking space lines. The parking spaces must be empty, by the way.

1. Start rolling downhill across the tails of the parking spaces. If there's no slope, approach with enough speed to slalom several lines nonstop.

2. Begin making Slalom Turns, with one carve around the tail end of the line, and the next carve up toward the head end of the parking space.

3. Make your centerline of travel as close as you can toward the head of the parking spaces, making sure you can still clear the tails. See how far beyond your centerline you can arc the alternate carves as well.

4. Keep your head and shoulders still and facing straight down the hill, but relax your waist and lower back muscles so that your hips can swing freely from side to side.

5. Flex deeply at the hips and knees (with torso upright) so your skates can extend further away from your centerline.

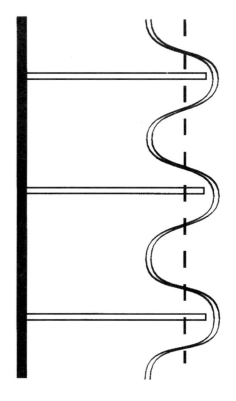

Upper body control

BEFORE YOU ROLL

Properly positioned arms help you make strong, complete turns and give your Slaloms stability and rhythm. When arms are not used properly, they will hinder your ability to turn and are more likely to throw you off balance.

1. Standing still in a relaxed ready position, raise your hands to waist level.

2. Raise your elbows so that they are at least six inches away from your waist, rounding out the shape of your arms.

3. Arch your back tightly (rear out). Feel how stiff your upper body has become. Varying degrees of this swayback position creep up on both skaters and skiers when they are tense, causing loss of mobility and flexibility to perform moves they can usually do with ease.

4. Now curve your spine in the opposite direction, rounding forward. Stretch it and then relax your spine, with hips slightly tucked forward.

5. Squeeze your shoulder blades together tightly on your upper back. Now separate them as far as possible, and watch how far your hands extend ahead of you without changing the way you are holding your arms. For skiers and skaters alike, reaching to make a pole plant down the hill should be done by extending from the wrist and shoulder blades, not by bending forward at the waist. Relax again.

6. Your rounded shoulders, arms and spine should be curved as if you're hugging a ball. This is the enhanced upper body ready position that is ideal for seriously fun downhill slaloms.

POINT TO THE TURN

With or without ski poles, the skier's arm position is an asset to the downhill skater. When the arms are properly placed, they affect the position of the upper body, which influences the pressured edging that controls your speed.

In the following drill, because we will be working on large-radius turns, the upper body will not be constantly facing downhill. For large-radius slaloms, the shoulders follow the line of travel.

1. Begin a series of slalom turns down your hill, with your arms positioned as practiced in the previous drill.

2. Starting a turn toward the left, use your right hand to point across your path to the place on the pavement where you want to start your next turn.

3. At the moment you transfer your weight to the left skate, use your left hand to

point at the site of your next new turn, on the far right side of your path.

4. Continue making large turns, keeping your hands raised and ready to point, always within your peripheral vision.

5. Repeat the drill but without actually pointing with a finger.

HAND AND SHOULDER PLACEMENT

The following drill demonstrates the proper hand and arm positions for skating both short- and long-radius Slalom Turns.

1. Position your hands as though you're gripping the steering wheel of a car. Now raise both elbows 3 to 4 inches.

2. Start downhill in tight Slalom Turns.

3. **For short turns**, your hands (gripping the invisible steering wheel) will follow the centerline, with shoulders facing the bottom of the hill as your lower body sweeps smoothly from side to side.

4. Now make very large Slalom Turns.

5. **For long turns**, your hands and upper body will be aligned to rotate with your lower body as you round each curve, facing the flow of the turn instead of the bottom of the hill.

POLE TIPS

Skiers who cross-train on in-lines, as well as non skiing skaters, find that using ski poles adds confidence and a feeling of security on steeper hills. For this purpose, the poles are fitted with rubber-covered tips (search the Internet for "rubber tips ski poles").

If you're buying new poles just for skating, check out the mountaineering style poles that feature adjustable lengths and interior springs to decrease the jarring of ground contact. A cork grip adds to the comfort. These can be set to a longer length when used for Nordic style cross-country skating, or shortened for downhill slaloms.

Here are some poling basics.

• Grip the poles lightly, with pressure only at the fingertips.
• Keep hands in view, no more than 2 feet apart. Don't let them trail behind you.
• Use the ski pole to mark your rhythm. Tap it on the pavement directly in front of you the moment you shift your weight to the uphill skate to start a new turn.

- Do not jab the pole out in front of you; reach from the shoulder blades and flick it out by swiveling your wrist.

- Keep your chest facing ahead, not down. Bending at the waist makes it hard to keep your poles high enough to plant without jabbing.

- Keep your elbows slightly raised so that your arms are rounded.

Practice poling with this chapter's upper-body and hand-placement drills. This will help you properly initiate and complete your turns, maintain proper arm placement, and more effectively use your poles as a tool to improve timing and balance.

Mobility and balance drills

POLE PRACTICE

Set up some plastic cones (usually found at large sporting goods stores) about 15 feet apart in a line down your practice hill.

1. Start rolling from the top and begin making smooth Slalom Turns around the cones.

2. To initiate a turn to the left using poles, extend your left arm and wrist to lightly touch the pole tip to the pavement at the same moment you rise to shift your weight to the right skate. Then, as you roll past the stationary tip, keep the hand gripping the pole in front of your body. That hand moves forward with your line of travel; the tip remains where you tapped it.

3. To turn right, reach down the hill and tap with the right pole at the moment of weight shift.

4. Begin each turn with a pole plant well before you reach the cone you are turning around. Since you will be halfway around the turn by the time you pass the cone, both skates should be pointing straight down the hill as you pass it.

5. Vary your speed and turn size. Work on keeping both hands in front of your body where you can see them.

ONE-FOOTED SLALOMS

Here's a flat-pavement drill that improves your one-footed balance and mobility, and is also a great hip exercise. Incidentally, this can be done on either skis or skates.

1. Stride briskly to build up some speed on flat pavement.

2. Begin a series of fast, tight Slaloms. (See "Twister" on page 93.)

3. Once you've got a rhythm going, lift one foot and try to continue making tight turns on the other, balancing all of your weight on the one supporting skate as it snakes down the hill.

4. With enough practice you should be able to launch into a series of One-Footed Slaloms without the two-footed approach.

5. Practice until you can do this equally well on both legs.

CHAPTER 7

Getting Fit with Roll-Aerobics

Just imagine: Exercise with a smile! Even though in-line skating hardly feels like exercise, you reap fitness benefits whenever you commute to work, run errands, take a lesson from this book, or enjoy a rolling lunch break. This chapter guides you on a path toward improved aerobic fitness through skating.

Exercise benefits

The benefits of sustained aerobic exercise are well known: improved overall health, endurance and longevity. Better yet, 30 minutes of aerobic activity performed consistently six days a week can turn your body into a fat-burning machine in just three months. As your muscles get firmer and denser, you get stronger and increase your muscle mass. And the more mass you gain, the more calories you burn, even when you're asleep!

Of course, skating won't result in a body builder's physique, but, like running, it can contribute to muscle density on a smaller scale. Studies have shown that in-line skating delivers the same aerobic and calorie-burning benefits as running, as long as you keep the pace above 10 miles per hour. So whether you're still at the recreational level or already into Stride Three, a solid half-hour skate can still burn 200 to 400 calories.

Best of all, with the exhilaration and sense of freedom that comes with skating, sustained aerobics is not a problem because you probably won't be ready to quit after just 30 minutes. One day, it could be hard to make yourself stop and rest after two hours!

In-line skating is comparatively easy on your joints because the stride is made without a jarring footfall. Such low-impact movement is ideal for the worn joints of lifelong athletes and the increasingly brittle bones of aging exercisers. And because skating is weight-bearing, there's also the potential benefit of building up bone mass—a special concern for women, who face increased risk of osteoporosis in mid life.

Aerobic exercise puts most people in a great mood due to body chemicals called endorphins, which the body releases naturally through sustained muscular activity. The "endorphin high" is one of the best all-natural stress-reduction therapies around.

The more you exercise, on or off skates, the more likely you are to experience that high yourself. As you skate along, you'll notice that you're feeling particularly creative, happy or enthusiastic. If you're alone, you may find yourself inventing creative solutions to problems at work, or developing an entrepreneurial idea. To make the best use of such creative thinking, bring along a note pad and jot down your thoughts. When you get home, take action on your plans: don't let these unanticipated non-fitness benefits of your skating workouts slip away.

Guess where the inspiration for *Get Rolling* was born!

Training requirements

SKILL LEVEL

You will probably get a great workout the very first time you skate, simply because of poor coordination or nervous tension! Realistically, however, you can benefit from in-line exercise as soon as you've learned your basic Stride Two (page 74) and how to stop. After you develop your power stride, Stride Three (see page 95), you will be able to propel yourself through a workout at great speed with excellent overall muscle stimulation.

TIPS FOR SKATING IN THE WORLD
On a windy day, you can get a great workout on the "uphill" stretch against the wind, and then practice your Slalom Turns on the "downhill" stretch.

As a beginner, you won't feel comfortable with the speed of power strides, but that doesn't mean you aren't getting any exercise benefits. Check your heart rate while working through one of the lessons in the Beginning Skills chapter of this book and you are likely to find yourself in aerobic mode. After you have mastered the Beginning Skills, get out on a bike path and put in the hours to develop a confident Stride Two. Each time you skate, work on making stronger strokes and longer glides. Soon you'll be ready to learn a power stride.

After you have developed your power stride, there are ways to increase your stroke efficiency even further. Enroll in a Pilates class or get down to the gym for some strength training two or three times a week. Focus on the skate-specific muscle groups: abdomen, lower back, buttocks, thighs and calves. Because you also need to maintain a balanced physique, don't forget to work the muscles of the upper body, too. To round out your strength, flexibility and balance training, add Yoga. Find a starter Yoga program suited to the needs of skaters in the Appendix on page 137.

LOCATION

As long as the pavement is dry, you can get your skate workout outdoors. (See "Preparing for the elements" on page 40.) If you are lucky enough to have access to indoor skating, you can laugh in the face of old Mother Nature during wintertime or on bad weather days. You'll be amazed at how much energy a body can expend on skates, even in that restricted environment.

For the best skate training, find a long route where you can maintain a 10mph or faster pace without interruption. This can be a bike path that doesn't cross busy intersections; a long, empty parking lot; or a smooth street in a business park that is deserted during the hours you want to exercise. It should be mostly free of debris, slick spots, broken pavement and other hazards.

If you train on a bike path, you must accommodate other trail users. As your powerful stride swiftly closes the gap between you and oncoming traffic, you may need to prompt those who occupy the entire width to clear the way. (How could a *roller blader* be going so fast?) To do so in a polite way, stand erect and tall, and if necessary, put your hands on your hips to get wide, too. Be sure to smile and say "thank you!" as you roll by. Approaching the same situation from the rear, call out a cheery "passing on your left!" when you're within earshot.

SKATES

For starters, whatever skates you currently own are fine for beginning a fitness training program. If they're heavy or slow, that only adds to the amount of effort you must put forth for each stroke, which increases your ability to burn calories!

If you intend to make skating a serious fitness endeavor, begin researching skates specifically designed for fitness purposes. You can choose from a wide-ranging selection of in-lines that feature improved boot comfort; a longer wheel base for greater stability at speed; taller, narrower wheels that result in better stroke efficiency; and, in some cases, five-wheel frames. Be aware (or beware!) that five-wheel skates do not come equipped with heel brakes.

Speedometers that mount on your skates can clock your current and maximum speed as well as miles covered, both cumulatively and for individual trips. Search for "skate computer" or "skate speedometer" on the Internet for the latest technology.

TAKE CARE OF YOUR SKATING "MACHINE"

Wear socks that wick away sweat to protect your feet, and remember beforehand to apply moleskin or tape to places where your feet have a tendency to get hot spots.

For long workouts (45 minutes or more) carry a pack-mounted hydration system so you can conveniently replace precious body fluids by sipping water every 15 minutes or so. For mid-workout snacks, carry an energy bar or a banana to help keep fatigue at bay.

Wear your protective gear. Besides the obvious safety benefits, it will gain you more respect and stroking space on the trail when you're dressed in the garb of the serious in-line athlete.

The warm-up

To prepare for your in-line workout, skate at a moderate pace for eight to ten minutes to get your blood circulating and warm up your joints. Some people like to stretch before exercising, but it is better to wait until after you have completed your warm-up, when the muscles are more elastic.

Your feet need to warm up, too, since they take a few moments to reach full circulation when encased in snug boots. If the blood headed their way can't get past tight buckles or laces, your muscles will let you know. In the beginning or after a skating layoff, your arches may start burning during the first 15 minutes; if they still tingle five minutes later, stop and refasten your skates.

A Roll-Aerobics Plan

TRAINING

Skate your training route in your best form at a speed of at least 10 miles per hour. To monitor your training speed, use your automobile's odometer (or a bicycle odometer) to measure the first mile of your route. When you can skate that mile in 6 minutes, you have achieved 10 miles per hour.

When and wherever you skate, you can calculate your *average* speed with this formula from *Fitness In-Line Skating* (see page 33):

> **60**
> **divided by total skating minutes**
> **times the distance in miles**
> **= average miles per hour.**

So if you skate a measured one-mile course in six minutes, you are averaging 10 m.p.h. (60 divided by 6 minutes is 10, multiplied by 1 mile is 10mph). A good first goal would be to skate your entire 10-mile course in 60 minutes (1 hour). To find the number of calories you burn per minute by body weight and m.p.h., visit Rollerblade's *Calorie Usage Chart* at http://www.rollerblade.com/fitness/calorie/calorie_usage1.html.

Make technique improvement a priority, so that you can begin to involve the entire body in your workout and maximize the benefits from each stroke. Work on the individual components of the power stride (aerodynamics, arm swing, stride angle and duration, and edging) until you can put it all together on the trail.

Understand that a fat-burning metabolism cannot materialize or be maintained without consistency. On skates or not, your body needs aerobic training 3-5 times per week month after month and year after year.

More than just an exercise routine, this is a fitness lifestyle. As inherently fun as skating is, some people who are obsessed with fitness will still tend to build a workout program that leads to unrealistic—and in the long-term, harmful—physical and mental demands. Don't trap yourself into a "more is better" regimen that will lead to guilt feelings, or worse, quitting the program altogether if you miss a few workouts.

To keep a long skate session stimulating (especially if your route is the same day after day) throw in a little stroke variety.

- Practice gliding or slaloming on one skate

- On a wide section of trail, skate half a mile using alternating crossovers (see page 106)

- When approaching intersections, slow down using Slalom Turns, T-drags, or snowplow-style A-frame turns, or try a One-Footed Heel-brake Stop (only when you're adept, of course!).

A FITNESS TRAINING BOOK

Fitness In-Line Skating, Human Kinetics, by Suzanne Nottingham, designer of the IISA's ICP Level III fitness certification program, and co-authored by Frank Fedel, a researcher at the Henry Ford Heart and Vascular Institute.

- Practicing front- or backward Swizzles and Half-Swizzles can add a whole new dimension to toning the hips and thighs.

- To enhance overall physical performance, add long and short sprints (also known as interval training) to improve cardiovascular and endurance capacity

- Time yourself on measured distances to improve your speed

- Train on a route with a long, persistent uphill grade.

MONITORING YOUR HEART RATE

The heart rate required to achieve aerobic training is 70-80% of your maximum possible beats per minute. To gain the benefits cited at the beginning of this chapter, this rate must be sustained for at least 30 minutes three to five times per week on a consistent basis.

While exercising, to find out what percentage of maximum you are working at, you can multiply the results of a 10-second count by 6 to determine if you're training within the aerobic range. The table on this page shows 10-second counts for both 70% and 80% of training ranges, listed by age from 15 to 65 years old.

Find your ten-second count

AGE	70% COUNT=	PER MINUTE	80% COUNT =	PER MINUTE
15	24	144	27	162
20	23	138	27	162
25	23	138	26	156
30	22	132	25	150
35	22	132	25	150
40	21	126	24	144
45	20	120	23	138
50	20	120	23	138
55	19	114	22	132
60	19	114	21	126
65	18	108	21	126

Courtesy of the American Heart Association

This chart is based *averages*. At 50 years old, I used the numbers for age 35 because I am not average, and it's likely you aren't either. Recognizing that, there is now a new formula for estimating maximum heart rate:

208 minus (0.7 times age)

The old, widely-published formula used to be *220 minus your age*. This new one allows for higher estimated maximum heart rates for older people. The two formulas intersect at age 40. Find out more and use the automatic calculator on the Get Rolling web site at http://www.getrolling.com/orbit/hrcalculator.html. When you enter your age, we calculate your max heart rate and training ranges for both the old and new formulas.

Getting Fit with Roll-Aerobics

These results still do not come close to my own measured maximum heart rate (above 190 beats per minute). I believe I just have a little bird-like pumper. The point is, we are all unique!

How can you get an accurate heart rate count during your skate work outs? Here are some tips to help you keep tabs on whether you're working too hard or not hard enough.

- There is an informal but commonly accepted way to determine if you're skating at an aerobic training rate while in motion. As you stride rhythmically at your fastest comfortable speed, you should feel slightly breathless, but still able to carry on a conversation, taking a breath no more than every three words.

- If you're in your 40s, here's a quick and dirty way to check if your heart is pumping at least at the minimum 120 beats per minute: With fingertips on your carotid artery (felt at the sides of your Adam's apple), count seconds with the well-known method "one-one thousand, two-one thousand, three-one thousand." Since 120 is twice 60, if you feel two beats for every one-second count, you know you're working hard enough.

- Purchase a heart rate monitor to easily check current heart rate and time how many minutes you spend at your training rate while skating.

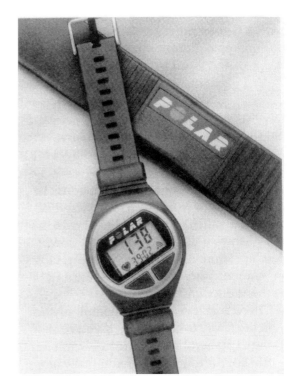

- You can also use a heart rate monitor to determine your actual maximum heart rate (with your doctor's permission) by gradually reaching an all-out sprint, preferably uphill after a half-hour aerobic workout. Set your training heart rates (70-85% of that number) accordingly.

Regardless of how you check it, if your heart rate seems too low, pick up your stroke rate and pressure, and swing both arms to involve your upper body.

Post-skate practices

When you're ready to call it a day after a hard workout on wheels, don't abruptly stop and kick off your skates. Ease out of your session. Take an extra five or 10 minutes to skate slowly or practice some skills or stunts. And when you do sit down to take off your skates, take the time to stretch while your muscles are still warm. Stretch your hips, quadriceps, hamstrings and lower back. Don't bounce; instead, use deep breathing. With each exhalation, the muscle being stretched will lengthen on its own. Some good post-skate Yoga stretches start on page 139.

Back on your feet, it may take another half hour to feel completely refreshed (and to stop shuffling your feet when you walk!).

Don't forget to recuperate after an especially hard workout by following it with a couple of days of easy skating, walking or no exercise at all. Drink lots of water right away (not soft drinks and not beer) and feed your muscles with a balanced selection of healthy foods.

CHAPTER 8

Great Places to Skate

Once you have perfected your stopping and speed control skills in that totally safe parking lot, more exotic locations await your exploration. Start with a flat bike path near home and build your confidence for future adventures and a fun in-line lifestyle.

Downtown skating. City ordinances vary for downtown skating, so ask at your local shop first. Parking structures are a typical skating favorite, but save these for night when there's less traffic and less chance of being asked to leave by security guards.

Be respectful of city property; if you aren't, you risk depriving us all of the privilege to skate the urban landscapes for fun, commuting or running simple errands.

> **TIPS FOR SKATING IN THE WORLD**
> Don't tempt thieves. Remove or thoroughly hide any valuables you must leave in your car when you go off to skate.

School yards: School yards are everywhere, and they're not just for beginners! After school hours and all summer long, school parking lots and paved playgrounds usually offer a variety of urban obstacles to challenge and inspire skaters of all ages. With a good mix of terrain, you can learn how to ride and jump short flights of stairs, make Slalom Turns, conquer curbs, and perform all manner of show-off tricks.

Newer neighborhoods: Today, many new housing developments offer smooth pavement, wide concrete sidewalks, and a neighborhood park with drinking fountains. The sweetest for skaters is a landscaped multi-use path that parallels, encircles or passes through the development. If your town has upscale "view lots" you can usually find prime hill skating in the neighborhood streets. Better yet, look for unfinished housing developments, where brand new streets are in but the homes are not up yet.

Bike Paths: These days, there are more places than ever to cavort alongside a creek, lake or park on the paved bike paths maintained by many cities and towns. Of course, bike paths must be shared with cyclists. Be courteous, control your speed, skate on the right side, pass on the left, and always pay attention to others.

When they extend out into rural areas, well-maintained paved bike paths are a prime spot for in-line touring. In some cases you can get a map of a town's paved bike-path system through the chamber of commerce, the bicycle transportation coordinator or the local visitor's bureau. On these maps, the Class One bike paths—dedicated paved trails with no automobile traffic—are what you're looking for.

The Web site of the *Rails-to-Trails Conservancy* is a great source for finding railroad beds that have been converted and often paved for recreational use across the United States. You can enter search criteria at http://www.railtrails.org.

Bike **Lanes:** Bike lanes, usually designated Class Two on bicycle commuter maps, are great for more experienced skaters. Someday, this could be you! Stay to the right when possible, but if you're descending a hill at the same speed as the traffic, take enough space to react safely to unforeseen situations. Use hand signals to make your intentions clear to motorists or to indicate whether they should pass you on the left.

When skating on the street, beware the overtaking motorist who suddenly cuts across your path to make a right turn. Your helmet and other protective gear, in addition to shielding you against injury, should serve as a red flag to remind such drivers that you're moving much faster than pedestrian speeds, but don't count on it. If you anticipate a possible "right hook," slow down and let the vehicle pass you, so you can maneuver around it rather than risk a deadly collision.

Beware: Legal restrictions for leaving the bike lane and entering the roadway can vary from city to city and may even be different for skaters than for bicyclists, so learn the score to avoid a citation.

Expect to skate

Bring your skates along on any trip, whether it's for business or pleasure, domestic or overseas. If you're a nature lover, don't forget to bring your skates along on car-camping trips so you can explore the roads and, if you're lucky, bike paths winding through the campground.

As long as you have skates and skills, you can explore just about any place that's paved at your own pace. Rolling among sights, sounds, and smells lets you fully experience the character of a quaint village or bustling city as well as the beauty of the countryside.

California In-Line Skating

If you live in or plan to visit California, be sure to visit the *California In-Line Skating* web site (www.caskating.com), which lists hundreds of skate tours rated for scenic beauty, pavement quality and required skater skills.

Skating the streets

In time, you will be ready, possibly even eager to take to the streets, whether it's to avoid the boardwalk crowds, commute on skates to your job, or explore a smooth country road.

The best streets for skating are those with light traffic, or with wide, marked bike lanes or shoulders. Remember that you are no longer a pedestrian when skating on the street. You are required to obey the same laws bicyclists do. For this reason, when road skating, skate in the same direction as the traffic near you.

Whether or not it has painted bike lanes, a road shoulder can be narrow, gravel-strewn, and basically unfriendly to in-line wheels. On the shoulders of country roads, watch out for intersections with driveways; they are often strewn with gravel.

If the road shoulder is narrow, you'll barely have enough room to stroke. Watch out for the foot on the traffic side. Ideally, keep your ears tuned and stop stroking when a car approaches. If you're climbing a hill, switch to swizzles when cars pass if necessary to avoid losing your momentum.

Stay alert to all that is happening around you. This means everything within your peripheral vision as well as in the direction you happen to be looking. Don't wear anything with earphones near traffic; you need to be able to hear as well as see.

> **TIPS FOR SKATING IN THE WORLD**
> A well-equipped pack for a long skate outing includes: water or sports drink, sunscreen, skate tools, energy bar, cash, ID and a miniature first aid kit.

Wide, empty streets with a downhill slope will surely invite Slalom Turn experts to connect asphalt carves across the width of a lane. (In some places, though, using the car lanes is not even legal.) If you hear a car horn honking angrily behind you, you aren't skating fast enough to be in its lane. Move to the side and let it pass.

Many urban areas hold guided weekend and week-night group skates. It's a fantastic way to meet and bond with other skaters in what becomes, to most participants, a positively euphoric experience! Usually, group skates are loosely-organized eight-to-20-mile affairs, often on city streets. Participants are responsible for their own safety and behavior, but helmets are typically required. Afterwards, some groups head to a local night spot for beverages and snacks.

Before you attend a group skate, find out where the route will take you and then check it out beforehand. If it's hilly, make sure you have solid speed-control and stopping abilities. Take a friend along when you join a group skate, because if you're at the back of the pack and take a spill, it's possible nobody will be around to help. Stick with the group (in skate-friendly cities, a group of 10-20 has enough mass to temporarily take over street right of way), obey the same laws

> **TIPS FOR SKATING IN THE WORLD**
> To keep tabs on automobiles when skating on the shoulder of a roadway, attach a rear view mirror to your sunglasses or helmet (available at most bicycle shops) or purchase a LookInBack ™ rear view mirror to wrap around one wrist guard.

motorists do, and don't skitch (allow an automobile to tow you). Bring along some money and an ID. It wouldn't hurt to carry your insurance card, too.

For nighttime skating, wear white or a reflecting vest or attach reflective patches to your clothing. It's also smart to wear reflectors or one of the flashing lights or head lamps that can be fastened to a helmet or belt; look for them at your local skate shop or outdoors outfitter. Wear all of your protective gear.

Access is in your hands

Every sunny day, this popular sport attracts hordes of skaters (along with pedestrians and cyclists) to the most popular boardwalks and bikeways around the country. Where congestion has become a problem, city governments have imposed speed limits or banned skating altogether.

You can help to prevent such restrictions by trying to make sure they're not needed. Learn to stop and maneuver safely in crowds, follow the posted regulations and limits, and skate with utmost courtesy, especially near pedestrians. If you like to skate fast, save it for early-morning or working hours or less-crowded locations.

Strive to improve your skills each time you skate. Use the lessons in this book to learn the downhill and street-skating techniques that are your passport to in-line adventures wherever you take your skates.

If your community starts to shut down skater access to bike routes or streets necessary for commuting, you can take action by following the advice on the International In-Line Skating Association's *Inline Skating Laws and Advocacy* page. See "Building Blocks for the Future" on page 32.

Congratulations!

You now are a *Get Rolling* graduate, joining millions of in-line skaters the world over! Having mastered all of the drills in this book, you may ask the same question I hear at the conclusion of some skating clinics, "So, what's next?"

There's a lot of fun and learning still ahead for you! I recommend you start with my second instructional book, *Advanced In-Line Skating*. You can buy autographed copies directly from me on the Get Rolling Web site (www.getrolling.com), operated by me and Web master Dan Kibler. The Web site also offers an archive of in-line skating articles written by both of us going back to 1992.

Write soon and share your stories, OK? liz@getrolling.com and dan@getrolling.com

Yoga for Skaters

BALANCE POSES

For best results, do balance poses on a hard floor with your gaze fixed on a stationary mark. To challenge yourself, do them on a plush carpet or on a wobble board. For less challenge, use a nearby wall for added support. Try to hold for 30 seconds or more. Start each pose standing as erect as possible with weight equally balanced over all parts of your feet (this is known as Mountain Pose).

Tree Pose (Vrikshasana)
- Press palms together in prayer position at chest
- Press right heel against left knee, with right knee and right heel turned out as much as possible
- (Optional) Raise right heel to left thigh (use your hands to pull the foot up if needed)
- Squeeze heel into thigh, pushing right knee back and hips forward
- If stable, raise hands overhead, palms facing in

Eagle Pose (Garudasana)
- Bring left elbow front and center
- Right elbow crosses under, backs of hands touch
- (Optional) Right fingers meet left palm
- Right knee crosses over left well-bent knee
- (Optional) Wrap right foot around left calf
- Lower limbs slowly and repeat on reverse side

BALANCE POSES (CONTINUED)

Warrior 3 Pose (Virbhadrasana 3)

- Raise both arms overhead, hands at shoulder width, palms facing in
- Extend right leg back, straight knee, toe on floor
- Tip torso forward as back leg lifts and balance on support leg without twisting hips or shoulders
- The ultimate pose is shaped like a capital "T" with a horizontal leg and torso
- Lower limbs slowly and repeat on reverse side

STRENGTH POSES

These poses build strength in the hips and both front and back of thighs. Try to hold each pose for one minute or more.

Bridge Pose (Setu Bandhasana)

- Lie on your back with heels close to hips, palms flat
- Starting with pelvis, roll spine slowly up off the floor
- Push hips and chest skyward; the neck stretches long
- Keep knees at hip width and hold steady
- Roll down one vertebrae at a time, starting with neck

Chair Pose (Utkatasana)
- Raise arms overhead, hands at shoulder width, palms facing in
- Bend both knees and stop before heels lift
- Distribute weight equally over fronts and backs of feet
- Fix gaze on a stationary point if balance wavers
- (Optional: Step one foot back into Warrior 1)

STRENGTH POSES (CONTINUED)

Warrior 1 Pose (Virbhadrasana 1)
- Assume Chair Pose
- Shift weight to left foot
- Reach right foot straight back and land with toes angled out at a distance that allows the heel to stay in contact
- Square hips and shoulders to front, even weight both feet
- Shift weight to left to return Chair Pose for other side
- Repeat on the opposite side

Warrior 2 Pose (Virbhadrasana 3)
- With feet very wide, raise arms to sides, palms down
- Look over the left shoulder; turn left foot to point left
- Turn toes of right foot toward midline 45 degrees Shift hips left and bend knee with torso upright
- Left knee stays aligned directly over ankle, not tipped forward, and not bent more than 90 degrees
- Rotate right knee out, not down
- Repeat on the opposite side

AFTER-SKATE POSES
These poses feel very good after a long skating session, and help open joints and loosen muscles that become tight by the work. Stretching while your body is still warm is the safest way to reduce the risk of injury and gain better range of motion.

Wide Angle Forward Bend (Parsarita Padottanasana)
- *Stretches the feet, calves, hips and back*
- With feet very wide apart, put hands on hips
- Stretch as tall as possible to lengthen spine first
- Fold forward at the hip creases, head heavy
- (Optional: Hands to ground if too intense)

AFTER-SKATE POSES (CONTINUED)

Child Pose (Balasana)
- *Releases and stretches the lower and mid back*
- Kneel on a mat or carpet and sit on heels
- Fold forward and touch forehead to the floor
- Reach hands back on floor, palms up beside hips

Downward Facing Dog (Adho Mukha Svanasana)
- *Stretches hamstrings, calves, feet, back and shoulders*
- From Child Pose, rise to all fours, feet at hip width
- Raise tailbone high, and align head, spine and shoulders to make a straight line from tail to fingers
- Push heels toward floor and keep legs straight

Pigeon Pose Variation 1 (Ekapada Rajakapotasana)
- *Stretches the outside and front of hip*
- From Downward Dog, pull right knee toward nose
- Set right foot down under left hip, then lower right knee
- Touch down with left knee; push it further back if possible while torso stays upright, facing front
- (Optional: Hips facing front, rest on elbows)
- Repeat on the other side

Dancer's Pose (Natarajasana)
- *Stretches hips, thigh, shoulders. Great for balance, too!*
- From Mountain Pose, raise right arm overhead
- Use left hand to capture the left foot behind
- Tip torso forward while raising left knee up behind
- Press left foot into hand without twisting body
- Ultimate is "T" shape: horizontal torso and thigh
- Repeat on the other side

About the Author

A fourth-generation native of California, Liz Miller is an in-line skating instructor living in the San Francisco Bay Area. She has been teaching beginners and experienced skaters alike since she published the first edition of *Get Rolling* in 1992. Besides "liberating" first-time skaters with braking skills, her other favorite forms of skating are ski-style downhill slaloms and skating for fitness and adventure on California's many paved routes. Liz also works as a writer and communications consultant specializing in information technology.

Liz's lifestyle has always embraced movement and nature's outdoor bounties. Besides in-line skating year-round, her summers are filled with hiking and backpacking, either in the nearby coastal hills or as high and far into the Sierra Nevada mountain ranges as free time allows. An expert alpine skier, she reserves most winter weekends for visits to the ski areas near Lake Tahoe. Entering the millennium, she adopted two new skate-enhancing passions, Yoga and Pilates.

When Ragged Mountain Press decided to discontinue the second edition of *Get Rolling* in 2002, Liz went back to her original self-publisher role because "I couldn't bear to think *Get Rolling* would no longer be available to help new skaters around the world!"

Other books by Liz Miller:

- *California In-Line Skating, The Complete Guide to the Best Places to Skate*. 1995, Foghorn Press (now out of print but available online at www.caskating.com)

- *Advanced In-Line Skating*, Ragged Mountain Press, 2000.

- *Sports and Recreational Activities*, 13th edition, by Mood, Musker and Rink, published by McGraw-Hill's text book division.

Liz has written articles for online skate tour web sites and various outdoors publications including *Northern California Hockey and Skating*, *Bay Area Parent*, *Fitness and Speed-Skating Times*, *New York Outdoors*, GNC's *Physical Magazine* and *On the Edge Magazine*.

Learn about Liz's latest skating tips, news, and fitness passions by visiting the Get Rolling web site at http://www.getrolling.com.

About the Author

Index